LL ELECTRONIC KEYBOARDS

ECTRONIC
EYBOARD
USIC®

MW00463797

FAVORITES

178

ISBN 0-7935-2175-0

Hal Leonard Publishing Corporation

7777 West Bluemound Road P.O. Box 13819 Milwaukee, WI 53213

E-Z Play ® TODAY Music Notation © 1975 HAL LEONARD PUBLISHING CORPORATION
Copyright © 1993 by HAL LEONARD PUBLISHING CORPORATION
International Copyright Secured   All Rights Reserved

Believe Me If All Those Endearing Young Charms

Regi-Sound Program: 9
Rhythm: Waltz

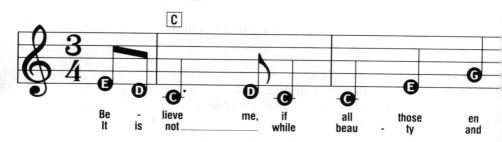

Be - lieve me, if all those en
It is not _____ while beau - ty and

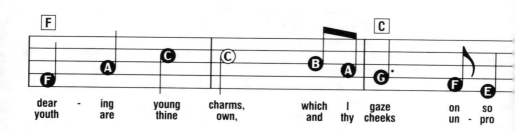

dear - ing young charms, which I gaze on so
youth are thine own, and thy cheeks un - pro

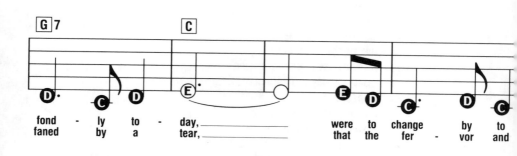

fond - ly to - day, _____ were to change by to
faned by a tear, _____ that the fer - vor and

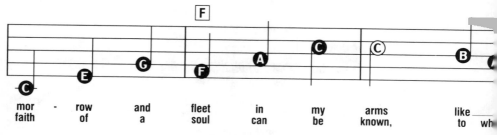

mor - row and fleet in my arms like _____
faith of a soul can be known, to wh

4

Danny Boy
(Londonderry Air)

Regi-Sound Program: 2
Rhythm: March or Polka

Words by E. Wea...
Music: Irish Tradi...

Oh, Dan - ny Boy, the pipes, the pipes are call - ing, _____ From glen to glen, and down the moun - ta... side. _____ The sum - mer's gone, and all the ros - es fall - ing. _____ It's you, it's you must go, and I mu...

5

The Galway Piper

Regi-Sound Program: 2
Rhythm: Rock or Pops

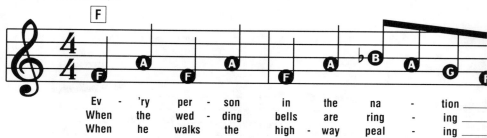

Ev - 'ry per - son in the na - tion _____
When the wed - ding bells are ring - ing _____
When he walks the high - way peal - ing _____

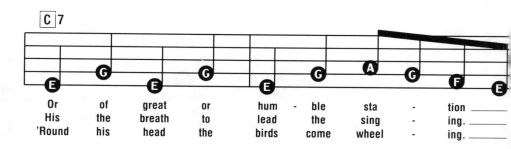

Or of great or hum - ble sta - tion _____
His the breath to lead the sing - ing. _____
'Round his head the birds come wheel - ing. _____

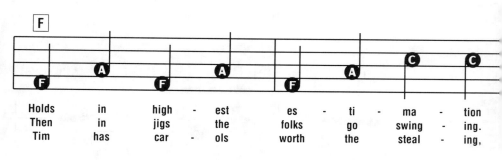

Holds in high - est es - ti - ma - tion
Then in jigs the folks go swing - ing.
Tim has car - ols worth the steal - ing,

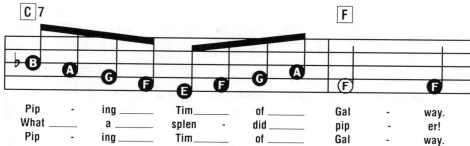

Pip - ing _____ Tim _____ of _____ Gal - way.
What _____ a _____ splen - did _____ pip - er!
Pip - ing _____ Tim _____ of _____ Gal - way.

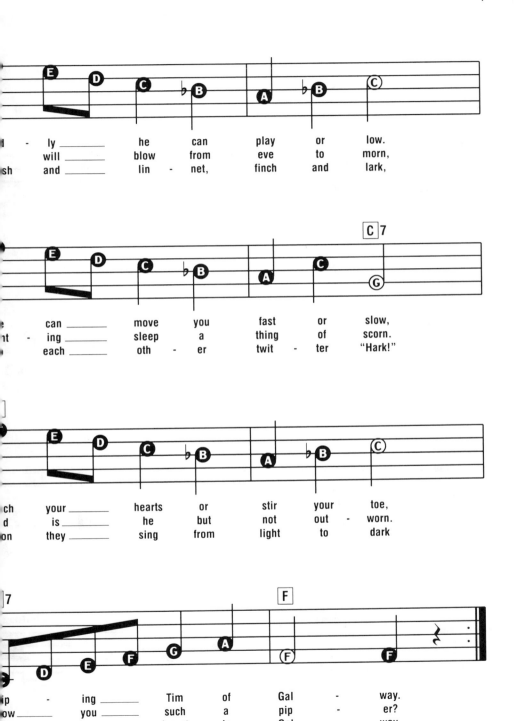

E D C ♭B A ♭B C

- ly _____ he can play or low.
will _____ blow from eve to morn,
sh and _____ lin - net, finch and lark,

C 7

E D C ♭B A C G

can _____ move you fast or slow,
- ing _____ sleep a thing of scorn.
each _____ oth - er twit - ter "Hark!"

E D C ♭B A ♭B C

ch your _____ hearts or stir your toe,
d is _____ he but not out - worn.
on they _____ sing from light to dark

7   F

D E F G A F F

ip - ing _____ Tim of Gal - way.
ow _____ you _____ such a pip - er?
ip - ings _____ learnt in Gal - way.

Garryowen

Regi-Sound Program: 9
Rhythm: 6/8 March

1. Let ____ Bac - chus' sons ____ be not ____ dis - mayed, Bu
2. - 5. *(See Additional Lyrics)*

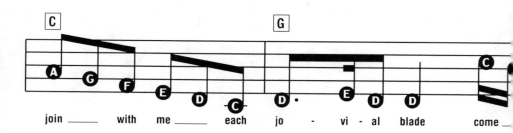

join ____ with me ____ each jo - vi - al blade come ____

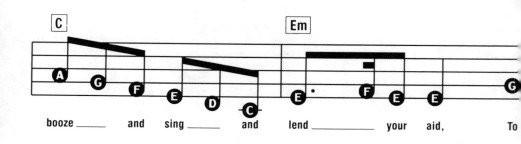

booze ____ and sing ____ and lend ____ your aid, To

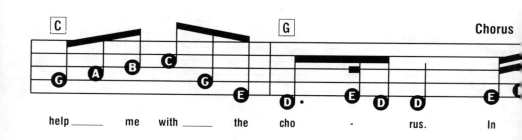

help ____ me with ____ the cho - rus. In

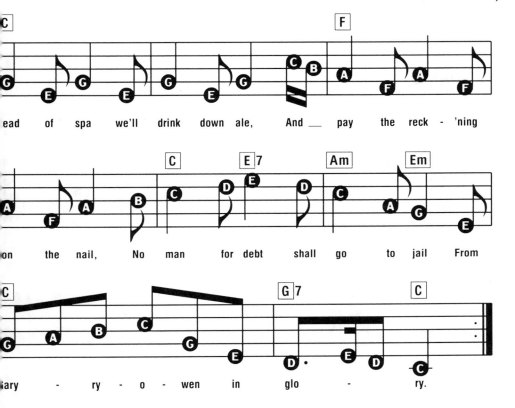

ead of spa we'll drink down ale, And ___ pay the reck - 'ning

on the nail, No man for debt shall go to jail From

ary - ry - o - wen in glo - ry.

Additional Lyrics

2. We are the boys that take delight in
   Smashing the Limerick lights when lighting.
   Through all the streets like sporters fighting,
   All tearing all before us.
   (Chorus:)

3. We'll break the windows, we'll break the doors,
   The watch knock down by threes and fours;
   Then let the doctors work their cures,
   And tinker up our bruises.
   (Chorus:)

4. We'll beat the bailiffs out of fun,
   We'll make the mayors and sheriffs run;
   We are the boys no man dares dun,
   If he regards a whole skin.
   (Chorus:)

5. Our hearts so stout have got us fame,
   For soon 'tis known from wence we came;
   Where'er we go they dread the name
   Of Garryowen in glory.
   (Chorus:)

The Girl I Left Behind Me

Regi-Sound Program: 10
Rhythm: Rock or Pops

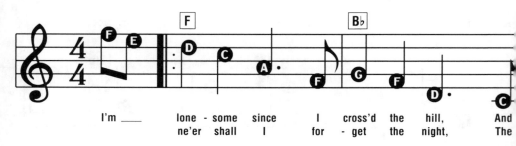

I'm ___ lone - some since I cross'd the hill, And
ne'er shall I for - get the night, The

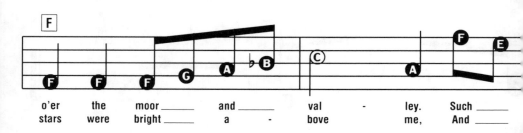

o'er the moor ___ and ___ val - ley. Such ___
stars were bright ___ a - bove me, And ___

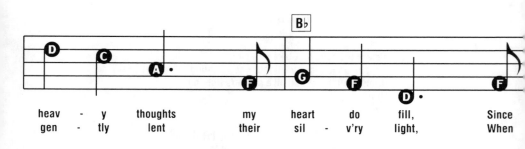

heav - y thoughts my heart do fill, Since
gen - tly lent their sil - v'ry light, When

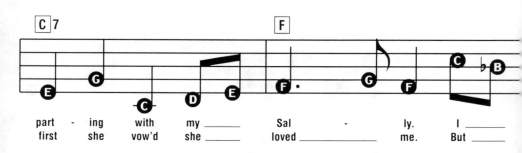

part - ing with my ___ Sal - ly. I ___
first she vow'd she ___ loved ___ me. But ___

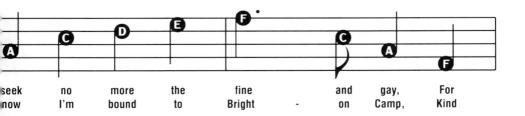

seek | no | more | the | fine | | and | gay, | For
now | I'm | bound | to | Bright | - | on | Camp, | Kind

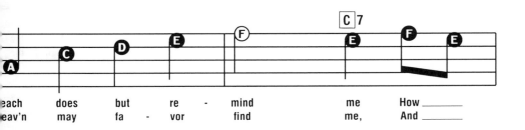

each | does | but | re | - | mind | | me | How _____
eav'n | may | fa | - | vor | find | | me, | And _____

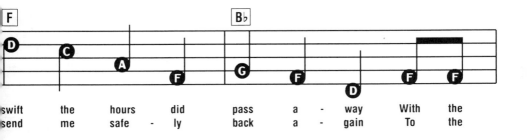

swift | the | hours | did | pass | a | - | way | With | the
send | me | safe | - | ly | back | a | - | gain | To | the

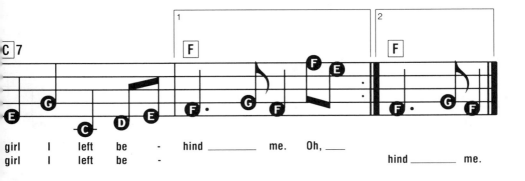

girl | I | left | be | - | hind _____ | me. | Oh, ___
girl | I | left | be | - | | | hind _____ | me.

The Harp That Once Thro' Tara's Halls

Regi-Sound Program: 3
Rhythm: Pops or 8-Beat

Words
Thomas Mo

The harp that once thro' Ta - ra's hall the
more to chiefs and la - dies bright the

soul of mu - sic shed, now
harp of Ta - ra's swells, the

hangs as mute on Ta - ra's walls as
chord a - lone, on that breaks at night, its

if that soul were fled. So
tale of ru - in tells. Thus

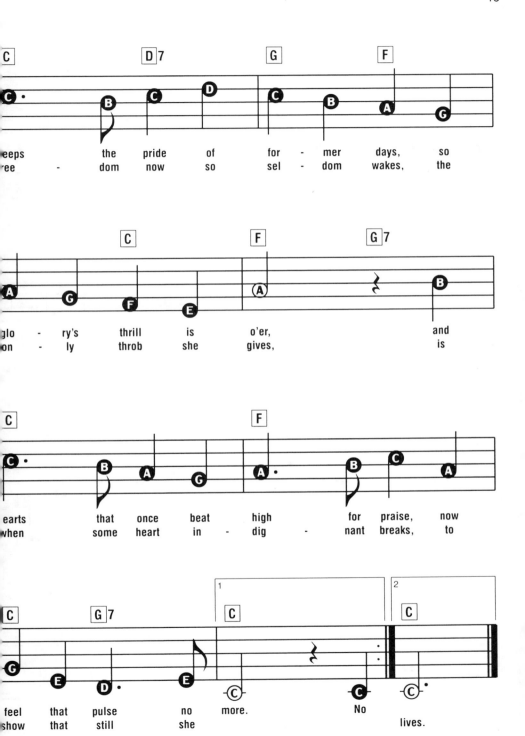

Harrigan

Regi-Sound Program: 5
Rhythm: March

Words and Music
George M. Col

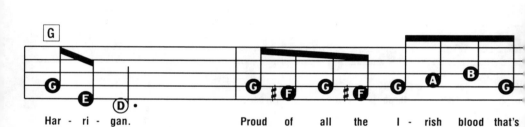

H - A dou - ble R - I - G - A - N spells

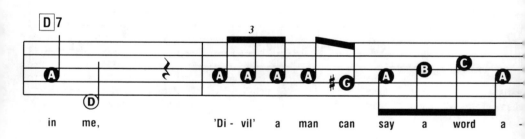

Har - ri - gan. Proud of all the I - rish blood that's

in me, 'Di - vil' a man can say a word a -

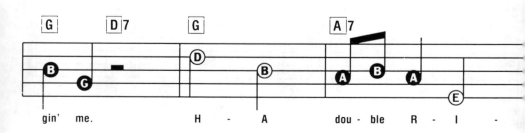

gin' me. H - A dou - ble R - I -

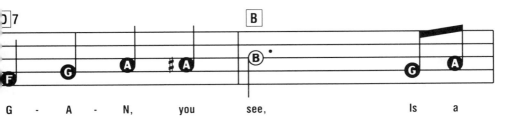

G - A - N, you see, Is a

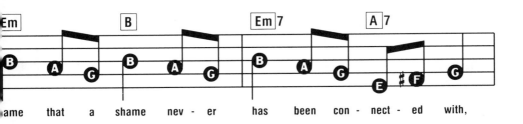

ame that a shame nev - er has been con - nect - ed with,

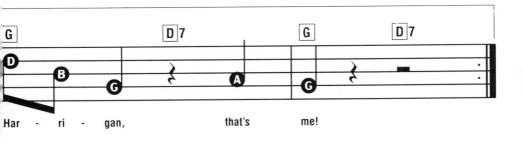

Har - ri - gan, that's me!

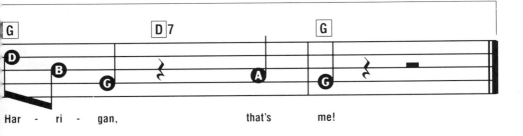

Har - ri - gan, that's me!

Has Anybody Here Seen Kelly?

Regi-Sound Program: 9
Rhythm: Swing

Words and Music
C.W. Murphy and Will Lett

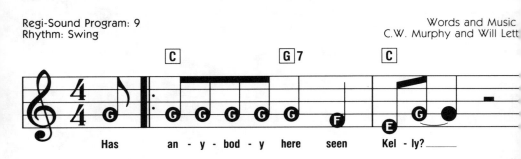

Has an - y - bod - y here seen Kel - ly?____

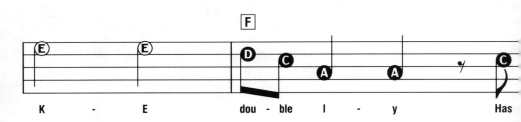

K - E dou - ble l - y Has

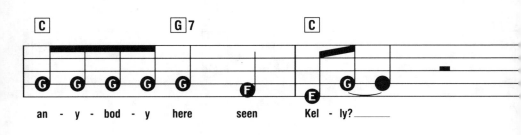

an - y - bod - y here seen Kel - ly?____

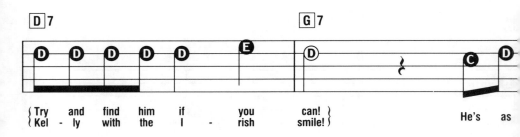

{ Try and find him if you can! }
{ Kel - ly with the I - rish smile! }
He's as

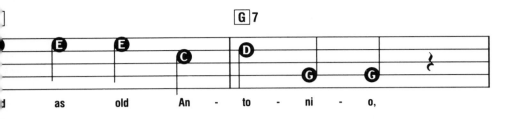

as old An - to - ni - o,

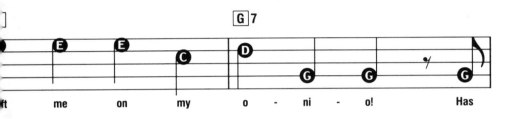

me on my o - ni - o! Has

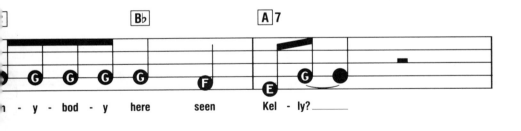

n - y - bod - y here seen Kel - ly?

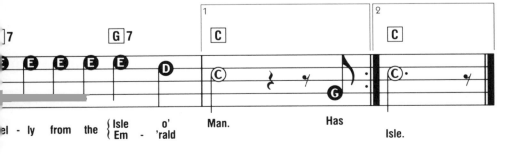

el - ly from the {Isle o' / Em - 'rald} Man. Has Isle.

If I Knock The "L" Out Of Kelly

(It Would Still Be Kelly To Me)

Regi-Sound Program: 8
Rhythm: Waltz

Words by Sam M. Lewis and Joe Yo
Music by Bert G

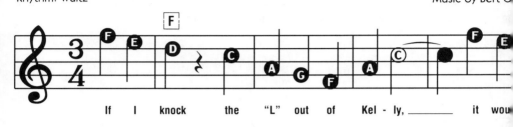

If I knock the "L" out of Kel - ly, _____ it wou

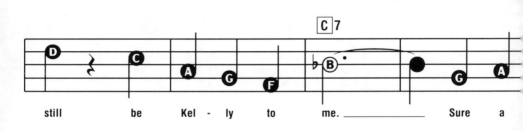

still be Kel - ly to me. _____ Sure a

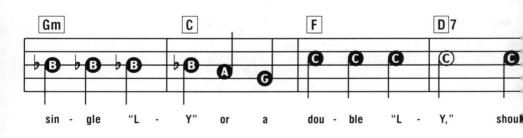

sin - gle "L - Y" or a dou - ble "L - Y," shou

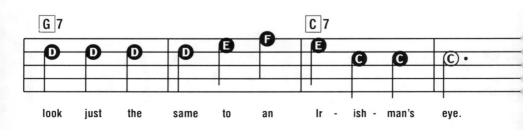

look just the same to an Ir - ish - man's eye.

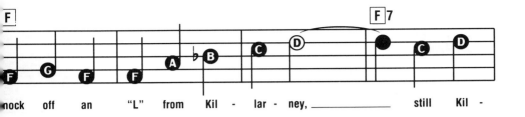

nock off an "L" from Kil - lar - ney, _____ still Kil -

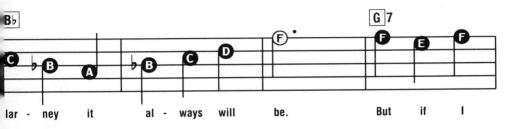

lar - ney it al - ways will be. But if I

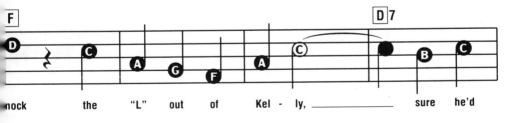

nock the "L" out of Kel - ly, _____ sure he'd

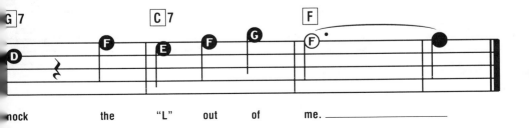

nock the "L" out of me. _____

Irish Washerwoman

Regi-Sound Program: 1
Rhythm: 6/8 March

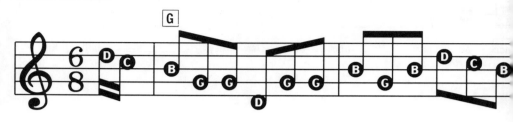

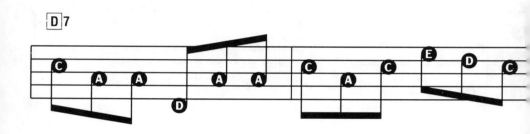

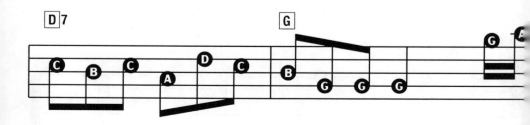

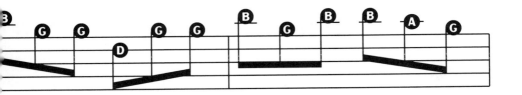

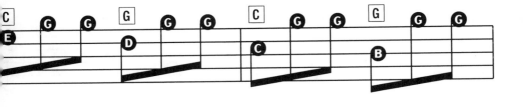

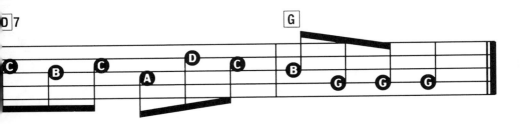

I'll Take You Home Again, Kathleen

Regi-Sound Program: 1
Rhythm: March or Polka

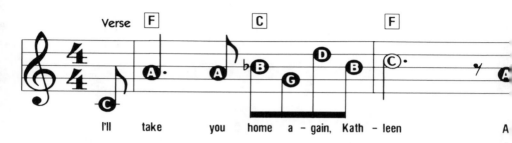

I'll take you home a-gain, Kath-leen A

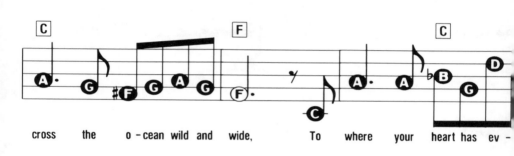

cross the o-cean wild and wide, To where your heart has ev-

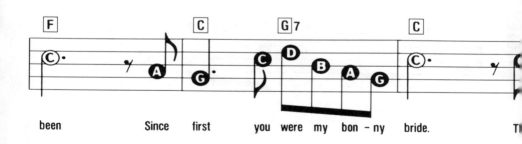

been Since first you were my bon-ny bride. T

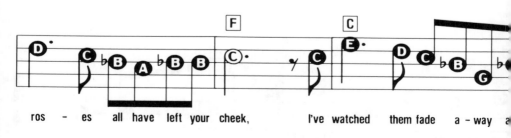

ros-es all have left your cheek, I've watched them fade a-way a

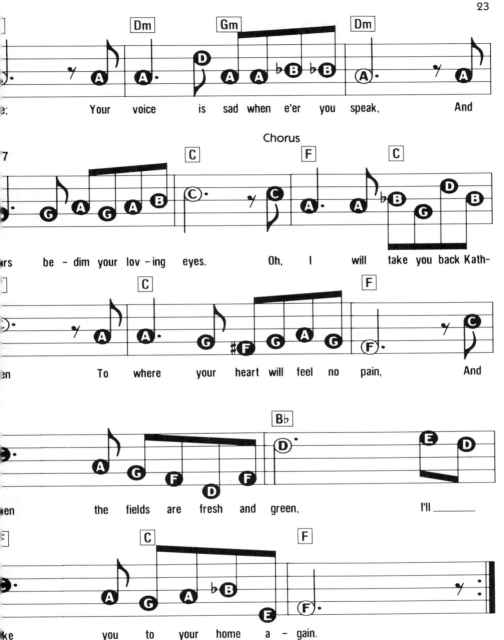

2. I know you love me, Kathleen dear,
Your heart was ever fond and true,
I always feel when you are near
That life holds nothing dear but you.
The smiles that once you gave to me,
I scarcely ever see them now,
Though many, many times I see
A dark'ning shadow on your brow.
CHORUS

3. To that dear home beyond the sea
My Kathleen shall again return,
And when thy old friends welcome thee,
Thy loving heart will cease to yearn.
Where laughs the little silver stream,
Beside your mother's humble cot,
And brightest rays of sunshine gleam,
There all your grief will be forgot.
CHORUS

The Kerry Dance

Regi-Sound Program: 2
Rhythm: 6/8 March or Waltz

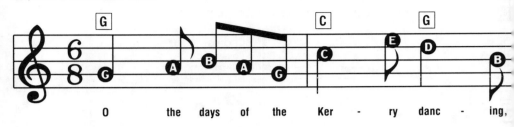

O the days of the Ker - ry danc - ing,

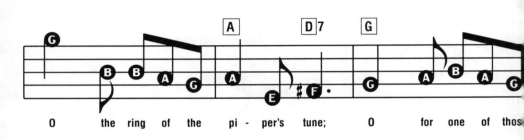

O the ring of the pi - per's tune; O for one of thos

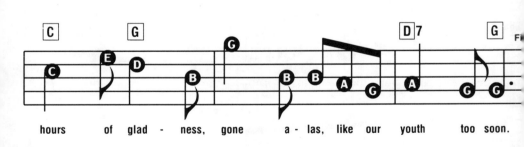

hours of glad - ness, gone a - las, like our youth too soon.

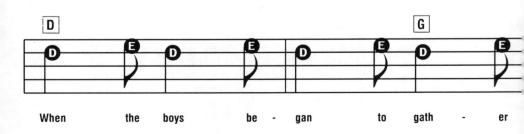

When the boys be - gan to gath - er

25

Killarney

Regi-Sound Program: 1
Rhythm: 8 Beat or Pops

Words by Edward Falco[...]
Music by Michael William B[...]

1. By Kil - lar- ney's _____ lakes and fells, Em - 'rald Isles and _____
2. *(See additional lyrics)*

wind - ing bays, Moun - tain paths and _____ wood - land dells,

Mem - 'ry ev - er fond - ly strays. Boun - teous na - ture

loves all lands, _____ Beau - ty wan - ders _____ ev - 'ry - where.

foot-prints leave on man-y strands, ___ But her home is ___ sure-ly ___ there! An - gels fold their wings and rest in that E - den of ___ the ___ west; Beau - ty's home, Kil - lar - ney, Heav - en's re - flex, Kil - lar - ney.

Additional lyrics

2. No place else can charm the eye
   With such bright and varied tints,
   Ev'ry rock that you pass by
   Verdure broiders or besprints.
   Virgin there the green grass grows,
   Ev'ry morn Spring's natal day,
   Bright hued berries daff the snows,
   Smiling Winter's frown away.
   Angels often pausing there
   Doubt if Eden were more fair,
   Beauty's home, Killarney.
   Heaven's reflex, Killarney.

Kitty Of Coleraine

Regi-Sound Program: 7
Rhythm: Waltz

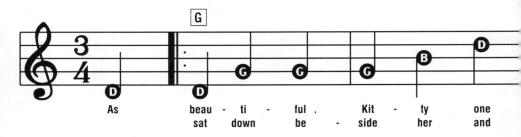

As beau - ti - ful, Kit - ty one
sat down be - side her and

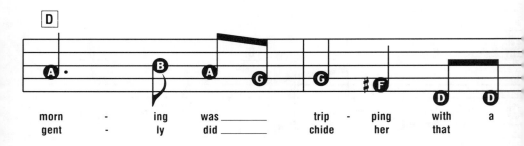

morn - ing was ____ trip - ping with a
gent - ly did ____ chide her with that

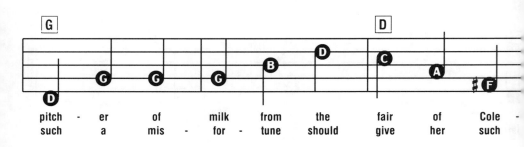

pitch - er of milk from the fair of Cole -
such a mis - for - tune should give of her such

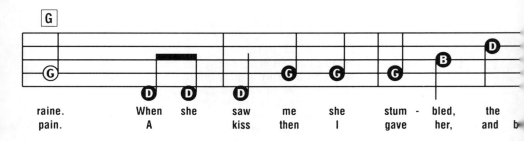

raine. When she saw me she stum - bled, the
pain. A kiss me then I gave her, and b

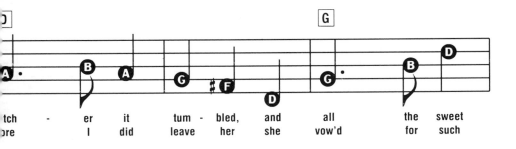

tch - er it tum - bled, and all the sweet
ore I did leave her she vow'd for such

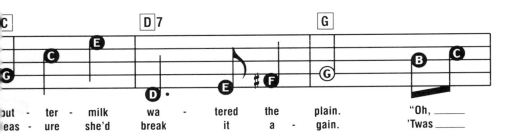

but - ter - milk wa - tered the plain. "Oh, _____
eas - ure she'd break it a - gain. 'Twas _____

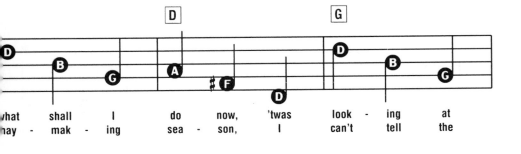

vhat shall I do now, 'twas look - ing at
hay - mak - ing sea - son, I can't tell the

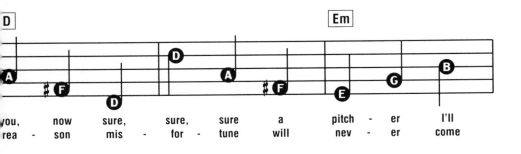

you, now sure, sure, sure a pitch - er I'll
rea - son mis - for - tune will nev - er come

30

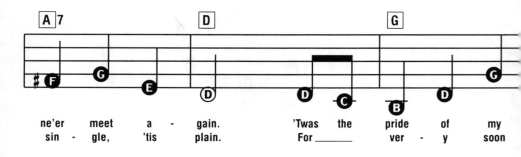

ne'er   meet   a - gain.   'Twas   the   pride   of   my
sin - gle,   'tis   plain.   For _____   ver - y   soon

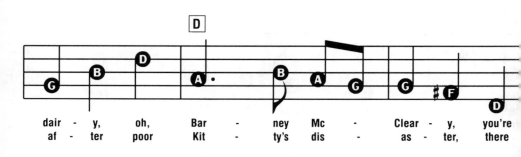

dair - y,   oh,   Bar - ney   Mc - Clear - y,   you're
af - ter   poor   Kit - ty's   dis - as - ter,   there

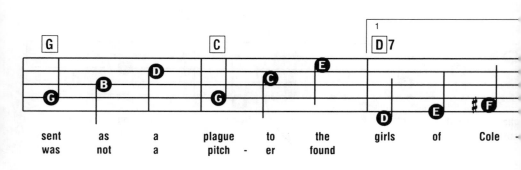

sent   as   a   plague   to   the   girls   of   Cole -
was   not   a   pitch - er   found

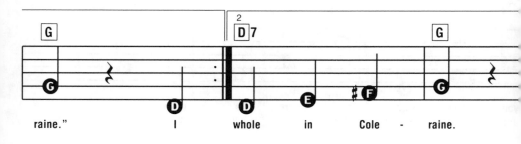

raine."   I   whole   in   Cole - raine.

McNamara's Band

-Sound Program: 5
hm: 6/8 March

Words by John J. Stamford
Music by Shamus O' Connor

Oh! me name is Mc - Na - mar - a, I'm the
now we are re - hear - sin' for a

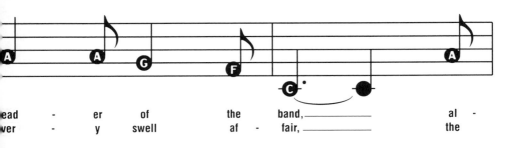

ead - er of the band, _____ al -
ver - y swell af - fair, _____ the

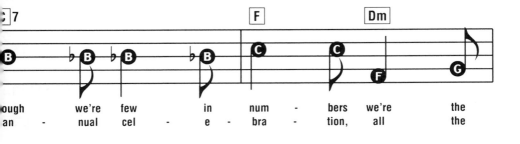

ough we're few in num - bers we're the
an - nual cel - e - bra - tion, all the

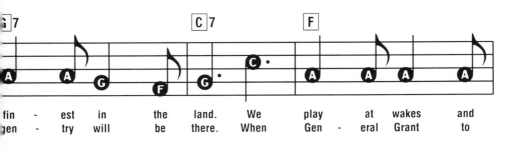

fin - est in the land. We play at wakes and
gen - try will be there. When Gen - eral Grant to

wed - dings and at ev - 'ry fan - cy ball,_____ and
Ire - land came he took me by the hand,_____ says

C7   F   Dm

when we play to fun - er - als we
he, "I nev - er saw the likes of

G7   C7   F

play the march from *Saul.* Oh! the
Mc - Na - mar - a's band." Oh! the

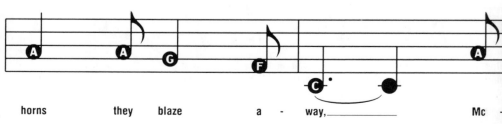

drums go bang, and the cym - bals clang, and the

horns they blaze a - way,_____ Mc -

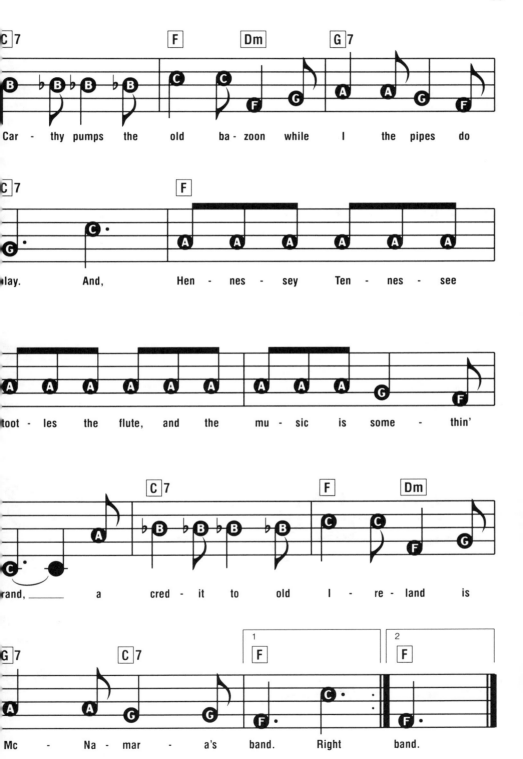

A Little Bit Of Heaven
(Shure They Call It Ireland)

Regi-Sound Program: 9
Rhythm: Slow Rock or Ballad

Words by J. Keirn Brer
Music by Ernest R. I

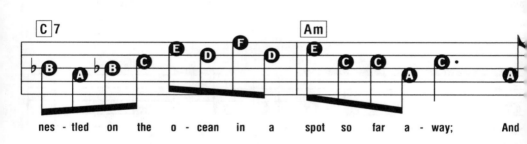

Shure, a lit - tle bit of Heav - en fell from out the sky one day, And ___

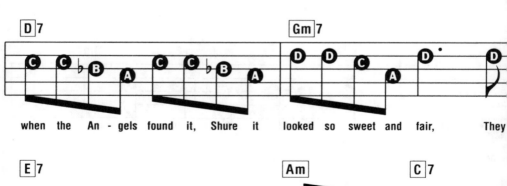

nes - tled on the o - cean in a spot so far a - way; And

when the An - gels found it, Shure it looked so sweet and fair, They

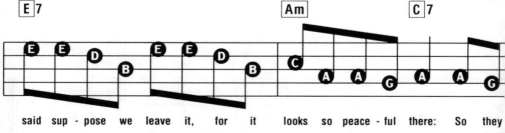

said sup - pose we leave it, for it looks so peace - ful there: So they

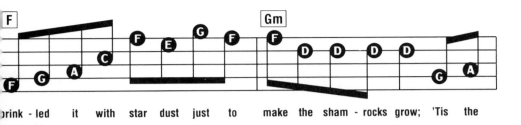

prink - led   it   with   star   dust   just   to   make   the   sham - rocks   grow;   'Tis   the

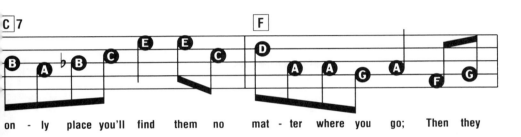

on - ly   place   you'll   find   them   no   mat - ter   where   you   go;   Then   they

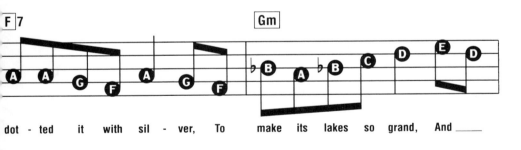

dot - ted   it   with   sil - ver,   To   make   its   lakes   so   grand,   And ____

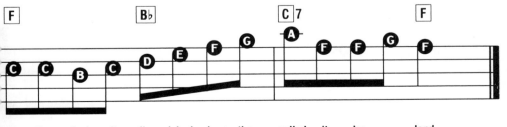

when   they   had   it   fin - ished   shure   they   called   it   Ire - land.

The Minstrel Boy

Regi-Sound Program: 3
Rhythm: March or Polka

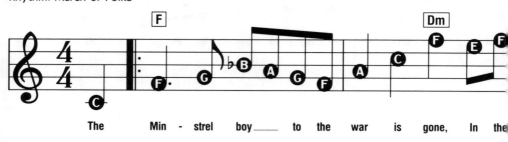

The Min - strel boy ____ to the war is gone, In the

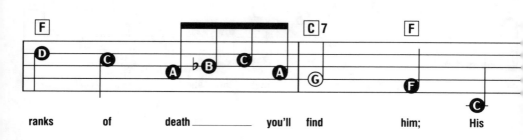

ranks of death ____ you'll find him; His

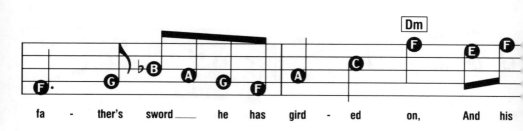

fa - ther's sword ____ he has gird - ed on, And his

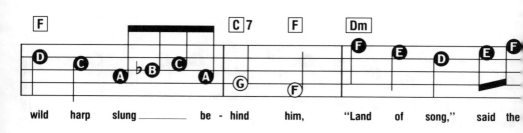

wild harp slung ____ be - hind him, "Land of song," said the

asy
ELECTRONIC
KEYBOARD
MUSIC®

The Biggest & Best Songbook Series
Created Especially for Electronic Keyboards!

- Custom designed for use with any keyboard.
- Convenient 6" x 9" format – books fit beautifully on the small, low music racks of electronic keyboards.

...ord notation used is compatible with the chording systems found in all electronic keyboards – no matter what brand.

...g-note single line music arrangements include chord symbols.

...e easiest music available for electronic keyboards – teaches anyone to play.

...ruction Books A & B
Instruction Books A & B are the fun and easy way to learn ...ay your electronic keyboard – no matter what brand!
...u'll Learn: • Music Basics • Keyboard Features • ...mpaniment • Fingering Techniques • Chords • ...ng Techniques.

...I Instruction Book A
...songs, including: Alley Cat • Don't Cry For Me ...ntina • Edelweiss • Memory • The Sound Of Music • ...Me Tender.
___00243367 ....$4.95

...I Instruction Book B
...ongs, including: Could I Have This Dance • Getting To ...w You • Just The Way You Are • Longer • Somewhere ...There • When I'm Sixty-Four • Yesterday.
___00243368 ....$4.95

...Supplementary Songbook
...pplement To EKM Instruction Books A & B
...1-filled songbook that lets you make use of everything ...learned in EKM Instruction Books A & B right away. ...a song is cross-referenced to the appropriate sections ...e instruction books.
Outstanding Songs Including: All My Loving • Stand ...le • It's A Small World • Let It Be • Hello Again • Fire ...Rain • The Rainbow Connection • Don't Cry For Me ...ntina • Earth Angel • When I'm Sixty-Four • and more!
___00243745 ....$4.95

...ette Instruction Course
...Easy Electronic Keyboard Music (EKM) Cassette ...uction Course is the "sound" way to learn to play any ...tronic keyboard! A comprehensive, easy-to-follow ...uction book is complemented by a "teacher on tape" – ...dio cassette that enhances the instruction book, further ...ains and demonstrates techniques and terminology and ...ides you with great songs to play-along with.
...e EKM Cassette Instruction Course Will Teach You:
...ic Basics • Keyboard Features • Accompaniment • ...ering Techniques • Chords • Playing Techniques.
...u'll Learn By Playing These Terrific Songs: Love Me ...der • Supercalifragilisticexpialidocious • Memory • ...weiss • Endless Love • Every Breath You Take • Just ...Way You Are • Could I Have This Dance • Yesterday • ...er • Somewhere Out There • and more!
___00243379 ....$12.95

Prices may vary outside the U.S.A.
Some titles in the series may not be available in ...ertain territories outside the U.S.A. Prices, contents ...and availability subject to change without notice.

Complete Instruction Course
The simple yet complete method that teaches you how to play and enjoy your electronic keyboard! Six comprehensive sections that cover: Basic Instruction (in two parts) • Exploring Automatic Rhythm • Exploring Playing Techniques • Exploring Intros & Endings • Exploring Chords.
Play These Great Songs While You Learn: Love Me Tender • Sunrise, Sunset • Feelings • Neutron Dance • Love Is Blue • Crazy • People In The Mood • It's A Small World • Could I Have This Dance • Can't Help Falling In Love • The Rainbow Connection • Endless Love • The Hawaiian Wedding Song • I Left My Heart In San Francisco • and many more!
___00243373 ....$19.95

Exploring Automatic Rhythm
A special supplementary edition teaching new techniques and various features of automatic rhythms on the electronic keyboard. Songs include: America • Can't Help Falling In Love • Neutron Dance • What Child Is This? • more.
___00243197 ....$4.95

Exploring Chords
A special supplementary edition teaching "fingered" chords. Includes 252 chord diagrams; explains what fingered chords are and how they are played; presents charts of the most common fingered chords for every note of the scale and in every position. Also includes 8 great songs: If You Remember Me • This Nearly Was Mine • Some Enchanted Evening • Love Is Here To Stay • Bewitched • I Left My Heart In San Francisco • Everytime You Go Away • In The Mood.
___00243198 ....$4.95

Exploring Playing Techniques
This book lets the electronic keyboard player in on "tricks" to further enhance his/her playing techniques. For example, it teaches the player how to add variety and interest to any song by changing registration, adding grace notes, etc. Songs include: Amazing Grace • And I Love Her • The Rainbow Connection • more.
___00243199 ....$4.95

Exploring Intros & Endings
This book reveals some of the secrets of the pros in creating introductions and endings for arrangements played on electronic keyboards. You can use these secrets to dress up and showcase your arrangements. "Exploring Intros & Endings" cuts through most of the technical material and gets to the heart of the matter, allowing you to apply the techniques learned right away. 11 songs, including: Can't Help Falling In Love • Bali Ha'i • The Hawaiian Wedding Song • Endless Love • People.
___00243196 ....$4.95

Exploring Double Notes

This supplementary book gives the keyboard player instruction on double notes, including the correct notes to play and how to come up with your own double note harmonies. It features 14 great tunes: Kumbaya • Yours • Don't Cry For Me Argentina • Somewhere Out There • The Entertainer • and more.

_____00290066..$4.95

Exploring Right Hand Chords

Exploring Right Hand Chords cuts through most of the technical material and gets right to the heart of how to add full chords to the melodies you play. A few basic principles are taught that allow anyone to sound good immediately.

_____00290248..$4.95

Exploring Backing Tracks

Experience the fun of overdubbing with your keyboard's sequencer! This book teaches how to read backing tracks in an arrangement, how to record backing tracks into a sequencer, and how to use backing tracks as duets to play live. 9 songs including: I Write The Songs • Somewhere Out There.

_____00244115..$4.95

DUET/BACKING TRAX

The arrangements in this series include both the melody and the rhythm line to popular collections of songs. You can play both parts with two hands, together with another player, or by recording the melody or rhythm onto your keyboard's sequencer and playing along with it. Great tunes make these books fun to play!

D1. Children's Songs

Over 20 songs to enjoy, including: Camptown Races • Humpty Dumpty • Hush Little Baby • Oh! Susanna • Old Grey Mare • On Top Of Old Smokey • Peter, Peter Pumpkin Eater • This Old Man • more.

_____00244103..$5.95

D3. Hymns

19 beautiful hymns, including: Amazing Grace • Crown Him With Many Crowns • Holy, Holy, Holy • Just As I Am • Onward Christian Soldiers • We Gather Together • much more.

_____00244105..$5.95

PLAY ALONG TRAX

Have you always wanted to play along with a professional band? With these great new book/cassette packs you can! These books come with a full band accompaniment cassette so you can play right along with the band and sound like a pro.

T1. Children's Songs

25 favorites to play along with, including: B-I-N-G-O • Camptown Races • Humpty Dumpty • Hush Little Baby • John Jacob Jingleheimer Schmidt • Oh! Susanna • On Top Of Old Smokey • Over The River And Through The Woods • Skip To My Lou • This Old Man • Three Blind Mice • more!

_____00244107..$10.95

T2. Christmas Songs

15 holiday favorites, including: Away In A Manger • Deck The Hall • The First Noel • Go Tell It On The Mountain • I Wonder As I Wander • Jolly Old St. Nicholas • Jingle Bells • Joy To The World • O'Christmas Tree • O Come All Ye Faithful • O Little Town Of Bethlehem • Silent Night • Up On The Housetop • more!

_____00244101..$10.95

T3. Contemporary Hits

Play with the band to eight favorite hits: Candle In Wind • Can't Smile Without You • I Write The Son Kokomo • Longer • Lost In Your Eyes • Somewhere There • What A Wonderful World.

_____00244108..$1

T4. Singalong Favorites

Everyone will enjoy these 15 classic singalongs: Bicycle For Two • Give My Regards To Broadway • Let Me Call Sweetheart • Take Me Out To The Ballgame • much m

_____00244100..$1

T5. Broadway's Best

10 of Broadway's absolute best, including: All I Ask Of • Climb Ev'ry Mountain • Don't Cry For Me Argentin Dreamed A Dream • Memory • My Favorite Things • S Of Music.

_____00244109..$1

T6. Country Standards

12 songs from your favorite country stars, including: Fall In Love Again • Forever And Ever Amen • God The U.S.A. • I Fall To Pieces • King Of The Road • R Top • Heartbreak Hotel • more.

_____00244114..$1

SONGBOOKS

1. Classics

31 selections including: Also Sprach Zarathust Andante • Barcolle • Blue Danube Waltz • Dance O Hours • Eine Kleine Nachtmusik • Fifth Symphony Mvt.) • Für Elise • Hungarian Dance No. 5 • Lar Minuet In G • Serenade • Theme From "Swan Lak "Unfinished" Symphony • Waltz Of The Flowers.

_____00243131..$

2. Standard Favorites

29 titles including: April Showers • Count Every Star Me A River • Daddy's Little Girl • The Exodus Song Foot Two, Eyes Of Blue • Harbor Lights • Here's Rainy Day • Imagination • Manhattan.

_____00243730..$

3. Best Of Neil Diamond

19 songs: America • Cracklin' Rosie • Heartlight • Again • Holly Holy • Longfellow Serenade • Love On Rocks • September Morn • Song Sung Blue • S Caroline • Yesterday's Songs • You Don't Bring Flowers • and more.

_____00243148..$

4. Best Of Duran Duran

15 favorites: Girls On Film • Hungry Like The Wolf There Something I Should Know? • New Moon On Mo • Planet Earth • The Reflex • Rio • Save A Prayer • U Of The Snake • and more.

_____00243170..$

5. Michael Jackson – Thriller

10 songs: Baby Be Mine • Beat It • Billie Jean • The Is Mine • Human Nature • The Lady In My Life • Mu • P.Y.T. (Pretty Young Thing) • Thriller • Wann Startin' Somethin'.

_____00243386..$

Lionel Richie
songs: All Night Long (All Night) • Endless Love •
llo • Love Will Find A Way • My Love Penny Lover •
nning With The Night • Stuck On You • Tell Me Truly •
u Are • and more.
__00243642 ....$5.95

Love Songs
titles including: Can't Help Falling In Love • Can't Smile
hout You • Endless Love • Feelings • For All We Know
The Hawaiian Wedding Song • My Funny Valentine •
nrise, Sunset • Through The Years • True Love • When
all In Love • You Needed Me • Your Song.
__00243453 ....$4.95

Beatles Greatest Hits
super hits: All My Loving • And I Love Her • Eleanor
gby • A Hard Day's Night • Hey Jude • I Want To Hold
ur Hand • Lady Madonna • Let It Be • Michelle •
rwegian Wood (This Bird Has Flown) • Ob-La-Di, Ob-
Da • Penny Lane • She Loves You • When I'm Sixty-
ur • Yellow Submarine • Yesterday • and more.
__00243061 ....$5.95

Good Ole Country
country favorites including: Any Time • Cold Cold Heart •
azy • El Paso • Green Green Grass Of Home • Heartaches
The Number • Heartbreak Hotel • Honey • Jambalaya •
g Of The Road • Little Green Apples • Make The World Go
ay • My Elusive Dreams • Your Cheatin' Heart.
__00243263 ....$4.95

. Broadway Spectacular
show tunes: Consider Yourself • Day By Day • Edelweiss
A Foggy Day • How High The Moon • I Could Have
nced All Night • If I Ruled The World • Just In Time • My
orite Things • Oklahoma • On A Clear Day • The Party's
er • People • What Kind Of Fool Am I • and more.
__00243078 ....$4.95

. The Sound Of Broadway
stage hits including: As Long As He Needs Me • Cabaret
Do-Re-Mi • Gonna Build A Mountain • I Love Paris •
e Grown Accustomed To Her Face • It Ain't Necessarily
• The Lady Is A Tramp • Memory • My Funny Valentine
The Sound Of Music • Try To Remember • A Wonderful
y.
__00243721 ....$4.95

. Hymns
selections: Abide With Me • Amazing Grace • Beautiful
vior • The Church In The Wildwood • Come, Thou
nighty King • Fairest Lord Jesus • Faith Of Our Fathers
Holy, Holy, Holy • Jesus Loves Me! This I Know • A
ghty Fortress Is Our God • Nearer, My God, To Thee •
ward Christian Soldiers • Prayer Of Thanksgiving •
ck Of Ages • In Jesus • and more.
__00243328 ....$4.95

. Jazz Standards
favorites including: Ain't Misbehavin' • All Of Me •
neysuckle Rose • Indiana • It's A Blue World • It's
ly A Paper Moon • Li'l Darlin' • The Lady Is A Tramp •
ve Is A Simple Thing • Lullaby Of The Leaves • Route 66
peak Low • They Can't Take That Away From Me.
__00243389 ....$5.95

14. Big Band Favorites
31 titles including: Bye Bye Blues • Charmaine • Cherokee •
I'm Confessin' That I Love You • In The Mood • Moonglow •
Moonlight And Roses • Opus One • Paper Doll • Pennies
From Heaven • Red Sails In The Sunset • Stompin' At The
Savoy • Things We Did Last Summer • Tuxedo Junction.
____00243066 ....$4.95

15. Country Classics
23 songs: By The Time I Get To Phoenix • Could I Have This
Dance • Wouldn't Have Missed It For The World • I.O.U. •
It's A Heartache • Luckenbach, Texas • Mammas, Don't Let
Your Babies Grow Up To Be Cowboys • My Heroes Have
Always Been Cowboys • Personally • Smoky Mountain Rain
• Somebody's Knockin' • Swingin' • and more.
____00243137 ....$4.95

16. Movie Song Classics
20 silver screen favorites: As Time Goes By • Born Free •
Can You Read My Mind? (Love Theme From "Superman")
• Chariots Of Fire • Days Of Wine And Roses • Jean •
Nine To Five • The Rose • (Theme From) A Summer
Place • Tara's Theme (My Own True Love) • Up Where
We Belong • The Way We Were • and more.
____00243501 ....$5.95

18. Hits Of The 80's
20 chart-toppers: Every Breath You Take • Flashdance…
What A Feeling • I Guess That's Why They Call It The Blues
• Islands In The Stream • Lady • Love On The Rocks •
Maneater • Memory • (Just Like) Starting Over • Total
Eclipse Of The Heart • Woman • and more.
____00243303 ....$4.95

19. Singalong Time
35 crowd-pleasing tunes including: After The Ball • Auld Lang
Syne • Bicycle Built For Two • Bill Bailey • Give My Regards
To Broadway • Goodnight Ladies • Meet Me In St. Louis,
Louis • My Gal Sal • My Wild Irish Rose • Sidewalks Of New
York • Sweet Adeline • Wait 'Til The Sun Shines, Nellie.
____00243690 ....$4.95

20. Merry Christmas
20 holiday melodies, including: The Christmas Waltz • Frosty
The Snow Man • Jingle-Bell Rock • Let It Snow! Let It Snow!
Let It Snow! • Parade Of The Wooden Soldiers • Rudolph
The Red-Nosed Reindeer • Suzy Snowflake • and more.
____00243494 ....$5.95

21. Christmas Classics
31 yuletide favorites including: Away In A Manger (Mueller) •
Deck The Hall • The First Noel • God Rest Ye, Merry Gentle-
men • It Came Upon A Midnight Clear • Jingle Bells • Jolly
Old St. Nicholas • Joy To The World • O Christmas Tree • O
Come All Ye Faithful • O Holy Night • O Little Town Of Bethlehem • Silent Night • Toyland • The Twelve Days Of Christmas.
____00243127 ....$5.95

22. Children's Songs
44 songs including: Are You Sleeping? • Chopsticks • The
Farmer In The Dell • Hickory Dickory Dock • Humpty
Dumpty • Kumbaya • Little Bo-Peep • London Bridge •
Old MacDonald Had A Farm • Pop Goes The Weasel •
Ring Around The Rosie • Row, Row, Row Your Boat •
Skip To My Lou • Ten Little Indians • This Old Man.
____00243125 ....$4.95

3

23. The Police
23 hits including: Canary In A Coalmine • De Do Do Do De Da Da Da • Don't Stand So Close To Me • Driven To Tears • Every Breath You Take • Every Little Thing She Does Is Magic • King Of Pain • Message In A Bottle • Roxanne • Wrapped Around Your Finger.
_____00243620 ....$6.95

24. The Best Of Elvis Presley
30 classics including: Are You Lonesome Tonight? • Blue Suede Shoes • Can't Help Falling In Love • Don't • Don't Be Cruel • Hound Dog • It's Now Or Never • Jailhouse Rock • Kentucky Rain • Love Me Tender • Loving You • Return To Sender • Surrender • Teddy Bear (Let Me Be Your) • Viva! Las Vegas • Wear My Ring Around Your Neck • Wooden Heart.
_____00243181 ....$5.95

25. Bob Seger & The Silver Bullet Band
13 favorites: Against The Wind • Even Now • Feel Like A Number • Fire Lake • Hollywood Nights • The Horizontal Bop • Mainstreet • Night Moves • Nine Tonight • Roll Me Away • Still The Same • We've Got Tonight • You'll Accomp'ny Me.
_____00243670 ....$4.95

26. Super Chartbusters
17 chart toppers: Careless Whisper • Hold Me Now • Left In The Dark • Missing You • Sad Songs (Say So Much) • Say Say Say • Sea Of Love • Sister Christian • Valotte • Wake Me Up Before You Go-Go • The Wild Boys • and more.
_____00243736 ....$4.95

27. The Best Of Carole King
19 songs including: I Feel The Earth Move • It's Going To Take Some Time • It's Too Late • Jazzman • The Locomotion • (You Make Me Feel) Like A Natural Woman • One Fine Day • So Far Away • Sweet Seasons • You've Got A Friend.
_____00243407 ....$4.95

28. Jumbo Songbook
103 songs from 7 categories: American Patriotic Songs • Classical Themes • Hymns and Sacred Songs • International Folk Songs • Polkas • Singalongs • Waltzes.
_____00243395 Plastic Comb Binding $12.95

29. Wham!
10 Songs: Bad Boys • Careless Whisper • Club Tropicana • Credit Card Baby • Everything She Wants • Freedom • Heartbeat • Like A Baby • A Ray Of Sunshine • Wake Me Up Before You Go-Go.
_____00243865 ....$4.95

30. Early Rock 'N' Roll
26 all-time favorites including: At The Hop • Blueberry Hill • Diana • Duke Of Earl • Goodnight, It's Time To Go • Hello Mary Lou • It's My Party • Johnny B. Goode • Lipstick On Your Collar • Save The Last Dance For Me • Sh-Boom • Shake, Rattle And Roll • Silhouettes.
_____00243173 ....$5.95

31. Super Pops
Songs: Don't You (Forget About Me) • Everytime You Go Away • Everything She Wants • Find A Way • Gloria • Hard Habit To Break • If You Love Somebody Set Them Free • Just As I Am • Neutron Dance • Nightshift • One Night In Bangkok • and more.
_____00243739 ....$4.95

32. Country Favorites
24 favorites including: Country Sunshine • Crackers • Crying Time • Everyday • God Bless The U.S.A. • Go Hearted Women • Islands In The Stream • A Little Go News • A Love Song • Ramblin' Man • Sail Away • Sleeping Single In A Double Bed • What's Forever For.
_____00243138 ....$4.

33. Listening Pleasure
24 classics: For All We Know • I Don't Know How To L Him • I Will Wait For You • If We Only Have Love Laughter In The Rain • Let It Be Me • Love Is Blue • M My Way • Please Come To Boston • The Promise • Sh Your Love With Me • Strangers In The Night • and more.
_____00243436 ....$4.

34. Jazz Favorites
22 selections including: Angel Eyes • A Foggy Day • I Ca Give You Anything But Love • Little Girl Blue • Lollipe And Roses • Moonglow • Satin Doll • Small World • String Of Pearls • Summertime • That's Life • Yesterday
_____00243392 ....$5.

35. Songs Of The 60's
26 songs including: California Dreamin' • Daydream Downtown • Georgy Girl • Groovin' • Happy Together It's My Party • It's Not Unusual • Monday, Monday • Love • One Tin Soldier • Shambala • Under T Boardwalk • Up, Up And Away.
_____00243706 ....$5.

36. Familiar Standards
28 all-time standards including: Around The World Bewitched • Boogie Woogie Bugle Boy • Come Rain Come Shine • Heartaches • I'll Never Smile Again • Li Girl • One Of Those Songs • September Song Sometimes I'm Happy • Sugar Blues • That's All • Th Coins In The Fountain • Too Young • Undecided.
_____00243208 ....$4.

37. Latin Songs
25 songs including: Call Me • Desafinado • Don't Cry I Me Argentina • Feelings • The Girl From Ipanema • Man And A Woman • Meditation • More • Poinciana Quiet Nights Of Quiet Stars • So Nice (Summer Samba) Spanish Harlem • Watch What Happens • Yours.
_____00243419 ....$4.

38. The Richard Clayderman Songbook
14 songs: Ballade Pour Adeline • Chariots Of Fire • Do Cry For Me Argentina • Harmony • Hello • How Deep Your Love • I Have A Dream • La Vie En Rose • Lar Theme • Love Is Blue • Love Story • Memory • Moon Riv
_____00243644 ....$4.

39. The Sound Of Music
7 selections from the motion picture including: Do-Re- • Edelweiss • My Favorite Things • and more.
_____00243680 ....$4.

40. Memorable Standards
27 favorite selections including: Bewitched • Everything Coming Up Roses • Falling In Love With Love • I've Got Y Under My Skin • Just A Gigolo • On The Street Where Y Live • P.S. I Love You • That's Entertainment • Till • T Close For Comfort • Under Paris Skies • Where Or When.
_____00243488 ....$5.

2. Soft Rock

[?] greats including: Crazy For You • Easy Lover • Even Now • [?]ven't Got Time For The Pain • A Horse With No Name • I'll [?]ve To Say I Love You In A Song • The Old Songs • Saving All [?] Love For You • Time In A Bottle • Welcome Back.

___00243695 ....$5.95

3. Walt Disney Favorites

[?] classics including: Bibbidi-Bobbidi-Boo • Candle On The [?]ater • Chim Chim Cher-ee • The Ballad Of Davy Crockett • [?]n Late • It's A Small World • Mickey Mouse March • A [?]oonful Of Sugar • Supercalifragilisticexpialidocious.

___00243858 ....$5.95

4. The Best Of Phil Collins – Updated

[?] of Phil's all-time best, including: Against All Odds • [?]nother Day In Paradise • Easy Lover • I Don't Care [?]nymore • I Wish It Would Rain Down • In The Air [?]night • One More Night • Something Happened On The [?]ay To Heaven • You Can't Hurry Love • and more!

___00243135 ....$6.95

5. Hot Pops

[?] songs: Election Day • Fortress Around Your Heart • [?]odbye • I'm Your Man • Miami Vice Theme • Sara • [?]e Built This City • You Give Good Love and more.

___00243309 ....$5.95

7. South Pacific

[?]li Ha'i • Happy Talk • I'm Gonna Wash That Man Right [?]uta My Hair • Some Enchanted Evening • There Is Nothin' [?]ke A Dame • A Wonderful Guy • Younger Than Springtime.

___00243685 ....$4.95

8. My Fair Lady

[?]et Me To The Church On Time • I Could Have Danced All [?]ight • I've Grown Accustomed To Her Face • On The [?]reet Where You Live • Show Me • With A Little Bit Of [?]uck • Wouldn't It Be Loverly.

___00243556 ....$4.95

9. Fiddler On The Roof

[?]o You Love Me? • Far From The Home I Love • Fiddler [?]n The Roof • If I Were A Rich Man • Matchmaker • [?]iracle of Miracles • Sabbath Prayer • Sunrise, Sunset • [?] Life • Tradition.

___00243213 ....$4.95

[?]0. Cats

[?]0 selections from the smash Broadway Musical, [?]cluding: Memory • Mr. Mistoffelees • Old Deuteronomy [?] The Old Gumbie Cat • and more.

___00243118 ....$6.95

[?]1. Barbra Streisand – Memories

[?]oming In And Out Of Your Life • Evergreen • Lost Inside [?]f You • The Love Inside • Memory • My Heart Belongs [?]o Me • New York State Of Mind • No More Tears • The [?]ay We Were • You Don't Bring Me Flowers.

___00243735 ....$5.95

[?]2. The Best Songs Ever – Revised

[?]ver 70 all-time favorites, including: All I Ask Of You • [?]andle In The Wind • Don't Know Much • Edelweiss • [?]ndless Love • Imagine • Let It Be • Longer • Memory • [?]omewhere Out There • Longer • Over The Rainbow • [?]nchained Melody • Your Song • and more.

___00243069 ....$12.95

53. The Best Broadway Songs Ever

Highlights: As Long As He Needs Me • Don't Cry For Me Argentina • Everything's Coming Up Roses • I Could Have Danced All Night • Camelot • Memory • Oklahoma • Old Man River • People • Sunrise, Sunset • The Sound Of Music • You'll Never Walk Alone.

___00243068 ....$12.95

54. The Best Country Songs Ever – Revised

Over 70 of the very best, including: Always On My Mind • Behind Closed Doors • Could I Have This Dance • Crazy • Daddy Sang Bass • D-I-V-O-R-C-E • Forever And Ever, Amen • Friends In Low Places • God Bless The U.S.A. • Grandpa (Tell Me 'Bout The Good Old Days) • Love Without End, Amen • Through The Years • and more.

___00243070 ....$14.95

55. The Best Easy Listening Songs Ever – Revised

Over 70 favorites, including: All Out Of Love • Blue Velvet • Careless Whisper • (They Long To Be) Close To You • Every Breath You Take • Hey Jude • How Am I Supposed To Live Without You • Lost In Your Eyes • The Rainbow Connection • Unchained Melody • Vision Of Love • Your Song • and more.

___00243071 ....$12.95

56. The Best Love Songs Ever – Revised

Over 60 sentimental favorites, including: Anniversary Song • Because I Love You (The Postman Song) • Don't Know Much • Endless Love • Here And Now • Just The Way You Are • Longer • Love Takes Time • Misty • My Funny Valentine • So In Love • Through The Years • You Needed Me • Your Song.

___00243072 ....$12.95

57. Barbra Streisand – The Broadway Album

11 songs from the smash hit LP including: Can't Help Loving Dat Man • If I Loved You • Send In The Clowns • Something's Coming • Somewhere.

___00243734 ....$5.95

58. The New Novelty Songbook

40 fun and silly songs, including: Chiquita Banana • Hello Mudduh, Hello Fadduh! • I've Got A Lovely Bunch Of Cocoanuts • Mah-Na, Mah-Na • Purple People Eater • Yackety Yak • Yes! We Have No Bananas.

___00243582 ....$7.95

59. Greatest Hits From The Movies

20 songs including: Candle On The Water • Endless Love • The Exodus Song • Flashdance... What A Feeling • Georgy Girl • Last Time I Felt Like This • More • The Rainbow Connection • Somewhere In Time • Theme From Ordinary People.

___00243273 ....$5.95

60. Rock Hits

17 rock classics including: Africa • Burning Heart • I Love Rock 'N Roll • Jump • Kyrie • Material Girl • Night Moves • Separate Lives • Slow Hand • This Is It.

___00243647 ....$5.95

61. Gospel Time

24 songs including: Build An Ark • Climb Ev'ry Mountain • He Did It All For Me • I Bowed On My Knees And Cried Holy • The Keys To The Kingdom • Lift Every Voice And Sing • One Little Step At A Time • Peace In The Valley • Salvation • Take My Hand, Precious Lord • Wings Of A Dove.

___00243267 ....$5.95

62. The Best Of Elton John
His 19 greatest including: Bennie And The Jets • Blue Eyes • Crocodile Rock • Daniel • Goodbye Yellow Brick Road • I Guess That's Why They Call It The Blues • Nikita • Philadelphia Freedom • Rocket Man • Your Song.
____00243394 ....$5.95

63. Favorite Singalongs
32 favorites including: Anchors Aweigh • Dixie • He's Got The Whole World In His Hands • Hello! My Baby • I've Been Working On The Railroad • In The Shade Of The Apple Tree • Just A Song At Twilight • Little Brown Jug • Oh My Darling Clementine • On A Sunday Afternoon • School Days.
____00243274 ....$4.95

64. Oak Ridge Boys Greatest Hits
20 songs including: American Made • Elvira • Fancy Free • Love Song • Make My LIfe With You • Ozark Mountain Jubilee • Sail Away • Thank God For Kids • You're The One.
____00243588 ....$4.95

65. Songs Of Inspiration
32 songs including: His Eye Is On The Sparrow • How Beautiful The Heaven Must Be • I Know That My Redeemer Lives • Jesus Savior Pilot Me • Jesus, Lover Of My Soul • Just A Closer Walk With Thee • Kum Ba Yah • Precious Memories • Shall We Gather At The River? • Softly And Tenderly • Sweet Hour Of Prayer • Were You There?
____00243705 ....$4.95

66. Alabama's Greatest Hits
22 of their best, including: The Closer You Get • Forty Hour Week (For A Livin') • Love In The First Degree • Mountain Music • She And I • and more.
____00243010 ....$5.95

67. Hawaiian Songs
29 island favorites including: Aloha Oe • The Hawaiian Wedding Song • One Paddle – Two Paddle • Red Sails In The Sunset • Tiny Bubbles.
____00243289 ....$5.95

68. Favorite Gospel Songs
23 songs, featuring: All Good Gifts • Day By Day • How Great Thou Art • Room At The Cross For You • and more.
____00243210 ....$4.95

69. The Best Of Hank Williams
25 of his best, including: Cold, Cold Heart • Hey, Good Lookin' • Honky Tonk Blues • I'm So Lonesome I Could Cry • Jambalaya • Your Cheatin' Heart • and more.
____00243875 ....$5.95

70. Christmas Favorites
19 holiday songs, including: Away In A Manger • The Christmas Song • I Saw Mommy Kissing Santa Claus • It's Beginning To Look Like Christmas • You Make It Feel Like Christmas.
____00243129 ....$4.95

71. Favorite Songs For Children
42 songs, including: Chim Chim Cher-ee • Happy Birthday To You • I Whistle A Happy Tune • The Muppet Show Theme • The Rainbow Connection.
____00243211 ....$5.95

72. Christmas With Kermit
21 Christmas songs, surrounded by illustrations of Kerm Songs include: Away In The Manger • The Birthday O King • Go Tell It On The Mountain • It Came Upon Midnight Clear • Up On The Housetop • and more.
____00243130 ....$4.9

73. Mickey's Christmas Favorites
23 holiday favorites, including: Auld Lang Syne • Deck T Hall • I Heard The Bells On Christmas Day • Joy To T World • O Little Town Of Bethlehem • We Three Kings.
____00243497 ....$4.

74. Top Country Hits
23 favorites, including: The Closer You Get • Grand (Tell Me 'Bout The Good Old Days) • I Believe In Me Talkin' In Your Sleep • You Take Me For Granted.
____00243780 ....$4.

75. Classical Themes
65 classic melodies, including: Brahms' Lullaby • Jes Joy Of Man's Desiring • Meditation • Romeo and Juliet William Tell Overture.
____00243133 ....$8.9

76. Patriotic Songs
23 songs of America, including: America • America T Beautiful • Battle Hymn Of The Republic • Star Spangl Banner • Yankee Doodle Dandy.
____00243596 ....$4.9

77. The Best Of Madonna
11 of Madonna's greatest: Angel • Borderline • Dress Yo Up • Everybody • Holiday • Like A Virgin • Live To Tell Lucky Star • Material Girl • Papa Don't Preach.
____00243467 ....$5.9

78. Singalong Fun
25 songs, including: Anniversary Song • Baby Face Edelweiss • Let Me Call You Sweetheart • Red Roses For Blue Lady • When Irish Eyes Are Smiling.
____00243687 ....$5.9

79. Simon And Garfunkel Greatest Hits
20 of their best, including: America • The Boxer • Brid Over Troubled Water • Cecilia • El Condor Pasa • Th 59th Street Bridge Song (Feelin' Groovy) • Mrs. Robinso • The Sound Of Silence.
____00243679 ....$5.9

80. 50 Super Standards
Songs include: Autumn Leaves • The Best Of Times • Her There And Everywhere • Johnny One Note • Midnig Cowboy • Music To Watch Girls By • Ol' Man River Sentimental Journey.
____00243214 ....$10.9

81. 51 Super Standards
Songs include: All At Once You Love Her • All My Loving Bye Bye, Love • (Ghost) Riders In The Sky • Hello, Doll • I Whistle A Happy Tune • Just A Gigolo • Misty • Put O A Happy Face • She Believes In Me • You Don't Bring M Flowers • You Made Me Love You.
____00243215 ....$10.9

52 Super Standards
gs include: C'est Magnifique • Everything Is Beautiful •
n't Give You Anything But Love • If I Were A Bell • The
g And Winding Road • Mame • Sail Along, Silv'ry
on • Satin Doll • Those Lazy-Hazy Crazy Days Of
mer • Yesterday • Zip-A-Dee-Doo-Dah.
_00243216 ....$10.95

53 Super Standards
gs include: Cherry Pink And Apple Blossom White •
o Again • I Have Dreamed • I Talk To The Trees • It
Almost Like A Song • Michelle • On Golden Pond •
es Of Picardy • Stompin' At The Savoy • Theme From
inary People • Unchained Melody.
_00243217 ....$10.95

54 Super Standards
gs include: Ballade Pour Adeline • Blue Velvet • Goin'
Of My Head • It's A Small World • Old Devil Moon •
Rainbow Connection • September Morn • Skylark •
ethin' Stupid • What I Did For Love • Who's Sorry Now.
_00243218 ....$10.95

Waltz Time
songs, including: The Anniversary Waltz • Edelweiss •
cination • Let Me Call You Sweetheart • The Most
utiful Girl In The World • Oh, What A Beautiful
rnin' • When Irish Eyes Are Smiling • Wunderbar.
_00243859 ....$7.95

Polka Time
songs, including: Beer Barrel Polka • The Merry
istmas Polka • Music! Music! Music! • Pennsylvania
ka • Too Fat Polka.
_00243621 ....$5.95

Marches
songs, including: Anchors Aweigh • Funiculi, Funicula
March Militaire • Stars And Stripes Forever •
shington Post.
_00243482 ....$5.95

The Big Book Of Disney Songs
songs, including: Bare Necessities • Candle On The
ter • A Dream Is A Wish Your Heart Makes • It's A
all World • Let's Go Fly A Kite • Mickey Mouse March
ome Day My Prince Will Come • A Spoonful Of Sugar •
ercali-fragilisticexpialidocious • When You Wish Upon
tar • Whistle While You Work.
_00243065 ....$16.95

Boogies Blues & Rags
favorites, including: Ain't Misbehavin' • Ballin' The
k • Basin Street Blues • The Entertainer • God Bless'
e Child • It Ain't Necessarily So • King Porter Stomp •
Man River • Stormy Weather • That's Life.
_00243075 ....$7.95

The Complete Wedding Songbook
songs of love and devotion, including: Could I Have This
nce • Endless Love • For All We Know • The Lord's Prayer
lay You Always • Sunrise, Sunset • You Needed Me.
_00243136 ....$9.95

91. Beatles Best
More than 120 songs, including: All My Loving • And I
Love Her • Blackbird • Come Together • Eleanor Rigby •
Get Back • Help! • Here There and Everywhere • Hey
Jude • I Want To Hold Your Hand • Let It Be • Michelle •
P.S. I Love You • Sgt. Pepper's Lonely Hearts Club Band.
_____00243057 ....$14.95

93. The Best Of The Judds
15 songs, including: Don't Be Cruel • Grandpa (Tell Me
'Bout The Good Old Days) • Rockin' With The Rhythm Of
The Rain • Why Not Me.
_____00243397 ....$5.95

95. The Best Of George Gershwin
27 songs, including: Embraceable You • I Got Plenty O'
Nuttin' • I've Got A Crush On You • It Ain't Necessarily So •
Let's Call The Whole Thing Off • Nice Work If You Can Get It
• S' Wonderful • They Can't Take That Away From Me.
_____00243250 ....$5.95

96. The Best Of Cole Porter
23 songs including: Begin The Beguine • Don't Fence Me
In • I Get A Kick Out Of You • It's De-Lovely • I've Got
You Under My Skin • Let's Do It • My Heart Belongs To
Daddy • Night And Day.
_____00243630 ....$5.95

97. The Best Of Rodgers & Hammerstein
More than 36 songs, including: If I Love You • Getting To
Know You • Hello Young Lovers • Oh, What A Beautiful
Mornin' • All At Once You Love Her • Bali Ha'i • Some
Enchanted Evening • Edelweiss • It Might As Well Be Spring.
_____00243650 ....$7.95

98. The Best Of Jerome Kern
29 songs, including: All The Things You Are • Can't Help
Lovin' Dat Man • The Last Time I Saw Paris • Ol' Man
River • Smoke Gets In Your Eyes • Why Do I Love You?
_____00243402 ....$5.95

99. The Best Of Marvin Hamlisch
15 of his best, including: The Way We Were • What I Did
For Love • One • The Last Time I Felt Like This • Smile •
They're Playing My Song.
_____00243282 ....$5.95

100. The Best Christmas Songs Ever – Revised!
A wonderful collection of over 90 classic and
contemporary Christmas favorites: All I Want For
Christmas Is My Two Front Teeth • Blue Christmas • The
Chipmunk Song • Do They Know It's Christmas? • Feliz
Navidad • Frosty The Snow Man • Grandma Got Run Over
By A Reindeer • Have Yourself A Merry Little Christmas •
It's Just Another New Year's Eve • Jingle-Bell Rock •
Rudolph The Red-Nosed Reindeer • Santa Claus Is Coming
to Town • Silent Night • and many more.
_____00243134 ....$12.95

101. The Best Big Band Songs Ever
69 great songs, including: Ballin' The Jack • Basin Street
Blues • Boogie Woogie Bugle Boy • The Continental •
Don't Get Around Much Anymore • In The Mood • Opus
One • Satin Doll • Sentimental Journey • String Of Pearls.
_____00243063 ....$12.95

102. The Best Of Barry Manilow
24 songs, including: Can't Smile Without You • I Made It Through The Rain • I Write The Songs • This One's For You • Tryin' To Get The Feeling Again • Weekend In New England.
_____00243473...$7.95

103. The Best Of Buddy Holly
19 of his best, including: It's So Easy • Maybe Baby • Peggy Sue • That'll Be The Day.
_____00243090...$5.95

104. The New Grammy Awards Song Of The Year
An updated edition that features every song named Grammy Awards "Song Of The Year" from 1958-1988. 32 songs, including: Volare • Moon River • The Shadow Of Your Smile • Up, Up And Away • Bridge Over Troubled Water • You've Got A Friend • Killing Me Softly With His Song • The Way We Were • You Light Up My Life • Evergreen • Sailing • Bette Davis Eyes • We Are The World • That's What Friends Are For • Somewhere Out There • Don't Worry Be Happy.
_____00243270...$9.95

105. The Best Of Billy Joel – Revised
23 of his best, updated to include his most recent hits. Features: And So It Goes • We Didn't Start The Fire • It's Still Rock And Roll to Me • Just The Way You Are • My Life • Piano Man • Tell Her About It • and many more.
_____00243073...$9.95

106. The Best Of Dan Fogelberg
15 of his greatest, including: Heart Hotels • Leader Of The Band • Longer • Part Of The Plan • Power Of Gold • Same Old Lang Syne • Twins Theme.
_____00243223...$5.95

107. Bruce Hornsby And The Range – The Way It Is
Matching folio to their smash hit LP. Featuring: Every Little Kiss • Mandolin Rain • The Way It Is • and six more!
_____00243307...$4.95

108. The Best Of Huey Lewis And The News
13 of their greatest hits, including: The Heart Of Rock and Roll • Hip To Be Square • I Want A New Drug • If This Is It • Jacob's Ladder • The Power Of Love.
_____00243323...$5.95

109. Kenny Rogers Greatest Hits
24 of his greatest hits, including: Coward Of The County • Don't Fall In Love With A Dreamer • Islands In The Stream • Lady • Lucille • Reuben James • Ruby, Don't Take Your Love To Town • She Believes In Me • Through The Years • You Decorated My Life.
_____00243660...$7.95

110. Christmas Carols
35 holiday favorites, including: Away In The Manger • Carol Of The Bells • Go Tell It On The Mountain • I Heard The Bells On Christmas Day • O Come All Ye Faithful • Silent Night.
_____00243123...$4.95

111. John Denver's Greatest Hits
A collection of his best. 24 hits including: Annie's Song • Back Home Again • Follow Me • Leaving On A Jet Plane • Poems, Prayers and Promises • Sunshine On My Shoulders • Take Me Home, Country Roads • Thank God I'm A Country Boy.
_____00243146...$7.95

112. Richard Clayderman – Hollywood & Broadway
Matching songbook to the album. 12 standards includ All The Things You Are • Embraceable You • If I Lo You • Night And Day • You'll Never Walk Alone.
_____00243155...$5

113. Queen's Greatest Hits
11 of their greatest, including: Another One Bites The I • Bohemian Rhapsody • Killer Queen • We Are Champions • We Will Rock You • You're My Best Frien
_____00243636...$5

114. Les Miserables
13 songs from the smash hit musical including: I Drear A Dream • In My Life • On My Own • Bring Him Hom and more.
_____00243425...$8

115. Barbra Streisand – One Voice
Matching folio to her album and television special. songs including: Evergreen (Love Theme From "A Sta Born") • It's A New World • Over The Rainbow • Pa Can You Hear Me? • Somewhere • The Way We Were.
_____00243737...$5

116. 25 Top TV Hits
25 songs from television, including: Dallas • The The From The Greatest American Hero • Hawaii Five-C Miami Vice • The Munsters Theme • Murder She Wrot Rockford Files • Secret Agent Man.
_____00243820...$5

117. Hits Of The 60's, 70's & 80's
46 incredible hits including: The Air That I Breathe • A When I Die • Dust In The Wind • Fire And Rain • H Habit To Break • Just The Way You Are • My Boyfrien Back • Rock On • September • Some Guys Have All Luck • Stoned Soul Picnic • Telephone Line • We're This Love Together • You Give Love A Bad Name.
_____00243300...$9

118. College Songs
31 favorite collegiate songs including: Caissons Go Roll Along • Fight On • Gridiron King • Hail, "Alma Mat • Notre Dame Victory March • On Wisconsin • Sweethe Of Sigma Chi • more.
_____00243139...$5.

119. The Gospel Songs Of Bill & Gloria Gaither
50 songs from this gospel due, including: Because Lives • The Family Of God • He Touched Me • The King Coming • Plenty Of Room In The Family • Someth Beautiful • more.
_____00243268...$9.

120. 55 Super Hits
Songs include: As Time Goes By • Chariots Of Fire • I L How You Love Me • The Rose • Sailing • Sweet Geor Brown • more.
_____00243219...$10.

121. 56 Super Hits
Songs include: Always On My Mind • Arthur's Theme Dancing In The Dark • Mack The Knife • Night And Day
_____00243220...$10.

122. 57 Super Hits
Songs include: Begin The Beguine • Bye Bye Blackbird • Fools Rush In • If • Nadia's Theme • Spanish Eyes • Up Where We Belong • The Way We Were.
_____00243222..$10.95

123. 50 Pop & Rock Song Classics
Songs include: Breaking Up Is Hard To Do • Cherish • Desperado • Goodbye Girl • It's Too Late • La Bamba • Life In The Fast Lane • Stairway To Heaven • Ventura Highway.
_____00243212..$10.95

124. 25 Top Hits Of The 80's
Songs include: Against All Odds • Always On My Mind • Back In The High Life Again • La Bamba • Moonlighting (Theme) • Who's That Girl • more.
_____00243816..$7.95

125. The Best Of James Taylor
23 of Taylor's best, including: Don't Let Me Be Lonely Tonight • Fire And Rain • Shower The People • Sweet Baby James • You've Got A Friend • more.
_____00243750..$6.95

127. The Randy Travis Songbook
20 songs, including: Diggin' Up Bones • Forever And Ever, Amen • On The Other Hand.
_____00243796..$5.95

128. Michael Jackson — Bad
Matching folio to the smash hit LP. 11 songs including: Bad • I Just Can't Stop Loving You • Man In The Mirror • The Way You Make Me Feel.
_____00243385..$5.95

129. The Songs Of Michel Legrand
40 of his best, including: Brian's Song (The Hands Of Time) • The Summer Knows (Summer Of '42) • The Windmills Of Your Mind • The Way He Makes Me Feel.
_____00243422..$8.95

130. Contemporary Country
23 songs, including: Forever And Ever, Amen •I'll Still Be Loving You • Love Will Find Its Way To You • To All The Girls I've Loved Before.
_____00243142..$5.95

131. Disney's Silly Songs
20 favorites, including: Little Bunny Foo Foo • Mairzy Doats • Ta Ra Ra Boom De Ay! • Be Kind To Your Web-Footed Friends.
_____00243153..$5.95

132. Folk Songs Of England, Scotland, Ireland & Wales
56 songs, including: Greensleeves • Scarborough Fair • Killarney • Londonderry Air • The Wearin' O' The Green • Auld Lang Syne • My Love Is Like A Red Red Rose.
_____00243230..$8.95

133. The Best Of Prince — Revised
Over 15 of his best, including: Cream • Delirious • I Would Die 4U • Kiss • Let's Go Crazy • Little Red Corvette • 1999 • Raspberry Beret • U Got The Look • When Doves Cry • and more.
_____00243632..$5.95

134. Amy Grant's Greatest Hits
21 of her best, including: Find A Way • Tennessee Christmas • Angels • El Shaddai • Doubly Good To You.
_____00243021..$5.95

135. Award Winning Songs Of The Country Music Association
More than 70 hits, including: Always On My Mind • Elvira • The Gambler • I.O.U. • Islands In The Stream • Lucille • Ode To Billie Joe • Rhinestone Cowboy • She Believes In Me • Southern Nights • Swingin' • Take This Job And Shove It • You Decorated My Life.
_____00243031..$14.95

136. Songs Of The 20's
56 songs including: Ain't Misbehavin' • Everybody Loves My Baby • Five Foot Two, Eyes Of Blue • Honeysuckle Rose • Look For The Silver Lining • Ol' Man River • Yes! We Have No Bananas • and more.
_____00243697..$10.95

137. Songs Of The 30's
58 songs including: All Of Me • A Foggy Day • In The Mood • My Funny Valentine • Pennies From Heaven • What A Diff'rence A Day Made • You're My Everything • and more.
_____00243698..$10.95

138. Songs Of The 40's
62 songs, including: Anniversary Song • Come Rain Or Come Shine • God Bless The Child • How High The Moon • Old Devil Moon • People Will Say We're In Love • So In Love • A String Of Pearls • The Things We Did Last Summer • You'd Be So Nice To Come Home To • and more.
_____00243699..$10.95

139. Songs Of The 50's
60 songs, including: All I Have To Do Is Dream • Blue Suede Shoes • Blue Velvet • Crying In The Chapel • Here's That Rainy Day • Misty • The Party's Over • Shake, Rattle And Roll • They Call The Wind Maria • Unforgettable • Young At Heart • and more.
_____00243700..$10.95

140. Songs Of The 60's
61 songs, including: As Long As He Needs Me • By The Time I Get To Phoenix • Dominique • The Girl From Ipanema • Hello Mary Lou • If I Had A Hammer • Love Is Blue • Monday, Monday • Our Day Will Come • Please, Please Me • That's Life • Those Were The Days • A Whiter Shade Of Pale • and more.
_____00243701..$10.95

141. Songs Of The 70's
49 songs, including: After The Love Has Gone • Daniel • Don't Cry For Me Argentina • Feelings • How Deep Is Your Love • Imagine • Joy To The World • Just The Way You Are • Laughter In The Rain • Let It Be • Mandy • Nights In White Satin • Send In The Clowns • Song Sung Blue • You Needed Me • and more.
_____00243702..$10.95

142. Michael W. Smith Greatest Hits
25 great hits from this very popular Christian singer/songwriter. Includes: Angels • Find A Way • Friends • How Majestic Is Your Name • Thy Word • To The Praise Of His Glorious Grace • and more.
_____00243693..$5.95

143. The Best Of Billy Ocean
10 of his best, including: Caribbean Queen • Get Outta My Dreams, Get Into My Car • Suddenly • When The Going Gets Tough, The Tough Get Going.
_____00243591..$5.95

144. Elvis Presley Anthology
59 songs, including: All Shook Up • Are You Lonesome Tonight • Blue Suede Shoes • Can't Help Falling In Love • Don't Be Cruel (To A Heart That's True) • Heartbreak Hotel • Hound Dog • In The Ghetto • Love Me Tender • Return to Sender • Suspicious • and more.

_____00243182 ....$10.95

145. Amy Grant – Lead Me On
Matching folio to the album. Features 10 songs, including: Lead Me On • Saved By Love • Shadows • Sure Enough • 1974.

_____00243022 ....$5.95

146. Faith – George Michael
Matching folio to the album. Nine songs, including: Faith • Father Figure • I Want Your Sex.

_____00243496 ....$5.95

147. 25 Chart Hits
25 chart-topping hits, including: Don't Worry, Be Happy • I'll Always Love You • Kokomo • Lost In Your Eyes • One More Try.

_____00290053 ....$6.95

148. Rock Revival
29 top hits from early rock era, including: Chantilly Lace • Don't Be Cruel • Louie, Louie • Splish Splash • The Twist • Wooly Bully.

_____00290054 ....$5.95

149. 25 Top Christmas Songs
25 of the best Christmas songs ever, together in one book Songs include: Do You Hear What I Hear • Have Yourself A Merry Little Christmas • Silver Bells • Sleigh Ride • Santa Claus Is Coming To Town • Here Comes Santa Claus • Frosty The Snow Man • and more.

_____00290058 ....$5.95

150. Bobby McFerrin – Simple Pleasures
Matching folio to the chart-topping LP. 10 songs, including "Don't Worry Be Happy" and "Drive My Car."

_____00290085 ....$4.95

151. Elton John Anthology
60 of his greatest, including: Bennie And The Jets • Crocodile Rock • Daniel • Goodbye Yellow Brick Road • I Guess That's Why They Call It The Blues • Lucy In The Sky With Diamonds • Philadelphia Freedom • Rocket Man • Sad Songs (Say So Much) • Tiny Dancer • Your Song.

_____00290102 ....$12.95

152. Songs Of The French Revolution
10 Revolutionary songs, including: La Marseillaise • La Carmagnole • It Will Come, It Will Come • Hymn To Voltaire • and others.

_____00290103 ....$4.95

153. The Best Of Eric Clapton
25 of this rock legend's greatest hits, including: After Midnight • I Can't Stand It • I Shot The Sheriff • It's In The Way That You Use It • Wonderful Tonight • White Room.

_____00290142 ....$5.95

154. Bangles – Everything
Matching folio to the LP. 13 songs, including: Be With You • Eternal Flame • In Your Room.

_____00290122 ....$4.95

155. Billboard Series – Best Of 1955
16 classics, including: Rock Around The Clock • Sixteen Tons • The Yellow Rose Of Texas • The Ballad Of Davy Crocket • Autumn Leaves • Let Me Go, Lover! • Dance With Me Henry • Hearts Of Stone • Unchained Melody • Moments To Remember • Earth Angel • Melody Of Love • Tweedle Dee • Only You (And You Alone) • Sincerely.

_____00290007 ....$5.95

156. Billboard Series – Best Of 1956
16 hits, including: Allegheny Moon • Blue Suede Shoes • Don't Be Cruel • Hound Dog • Heartbreak Hotel • The Poor People Of Paris • Memories Are Made Of This • Love Me Tender • My Prayer • I Almost Lost My Mind • Que Sera, Sera • True Love • No, Not Much • I Want You, I Need You, I Love You.

_____00290008 ....$5.95

157. Billboard Series – Best Of 1957
16 songs of yesteryear, including: All Shook Up • Butterfly • Chances Are • Honeycomb • Jailhouse Rock • Love Letters In The Sand • Peggy Sue • Tammy • Teddy Bear • Wake Up, Little Susie • Party Doll • That'll Be The Day • Too Much • Whole Lotta Shakin' Goin' On • Diana • Blueberry Hill.

_____00290009 ....$5.95

158. Billboard Series – Best Of 1958
15 golden oldies, including At The Hop • It's All In The Game • Purple People Eater • All I Have To Do Is Dream • Don't • Chipmunk Song • Get A Job • Great Balls Of Fire • It's Only Make Believe • Lollipop • Yakety Yak.

_____00290010 ....$5.95

159. Billboard Series – Best Of 1959
15 more classics, including: Mack The Knife • Battle Of New Orleans • Venus • Lonely Boy • Smoke Gets In Your Eyes • Heartaches By The Number • Sleep Walk • Kansas City • A Big Hunk Of Love • Why • Put Your Head On My Shoulder • Donna • Personality • Sixteen Candles • Charlie Brown.

_____00290011 ....$5.95

160. Billboard Songbook Series – Best Of 1960
16 songs: Alley-Oop • Are You Lonesome Tonight • It's Now Or Never • The Twist • Georgia On My Mind • and more.

_____00290013 ....$5.95

161. Billboard Songbook Series – Best Of 1961
17 songs: Hit The Road Jack • The Lion Sleeps Tonight • Moody River • Runaround Sue • Runaway • Blue Moon • and more.

_____00290014 ....$5.95

162. Billboard Songbook Series – Best Of 1962
15 songs: Big Girls Don't Cry • Breaking Up Is Hard To Do • Duke Of Earl • The Loco-Motion • Peppermint Twist - Part I • and more.

_____00290015 ....$5.95

163. Billboard Songbook Series – Best Of 1963
14 songs: Be My Baby • Blue Velvet • Go Away, Little Girl • It's My Party • Louie, Louie • My Boyfriend's Back • Surf City • and more.

_____00290016 ....$5.95

164. Billboard Songbook Series – Best Of 1964
14 songs: Can't Buy Me Love • I Want To Hold Your Hand • Leader Of The Pack • Rag Doll • and more.

_____00290017 ....$5.95

65. Billboard Songbook Series – Best Of 1965
7 songs: Downtown • Eight Days A Week • Hang On
Loopy • I Got You Babe • Yesterday • and more.
___00290019 ....$5.95

66. Billboard Songbook Series – Best Of 1966
5 songs: Good Lovin' • I'm A Believer • Monday, Monday
Summer In The City • Wild Thing • and more.
___00290020 ....$5.95

67. Billboard Songbook Series – Best Of 1967
7 songs: Daydream Believer • Georgy Girl • Happy
Together • Penny Lane • San Francisco (Be Sure To Wear
Flowers In Your Hair) • more.
___00290021 ....$5.95

68. Billboard Songbook Series – Best Of 1968
8 songs: Born To Be Wild • Harper Valley P.T.A • Hey Jude
Judy In Disguise (With Glasses) • Mrs. Robinson • more.
___00290022 ....$5.95

69. Billboard Songbook Series – Best Of 1969
9 songs: Come Together • Crimson & Clover • Get Back
Hawaii Five-o • In The Year 2525 • Leaving On A Jet
Plane • Sweet Caroline • more.
___00290023 ....$5.95

75. The Wizard Of Oz
A wonderful souvenir folio of photos, essays and 10 classic
songs from this timeless film. Titles include: Over The
Rainbow • Ding-Dong The Witch Is Dead! • The Jitterbug
We're Off To See The Wizard • and more.
___00243140 ....$5.95

76. Great Movie Songs Of Today
Over 25 songs, including: Beauty And The Beast • (Everything I
Do) I Do It For You • Kokomo • Somewhere Out There •
Unchained Melody • The Wind Beneath My Wings • and more.
___00243149 ....$8.95

77. Achy Breaky Heart & Other Country Chartbusters
5 top country hits, including the title song and: Boot
Scootin' Boogie • Gone As A Girl Can Get • I Feel Lucky •
Saw The Light • She Is His Only Need • Straight Tequila
Night • and more.
___00243145 ....$5.95

91. The Best Of Air Supply
11 songs from this superstar pop duo. Includes: All Out Of
Love • Even The Nights Are Better • Every Woman In The
World • Here I Am • Lost In Love • Making Love Out Of
Nothing At All • The One That You Love • and more.
___00290217 ....$4.95

92. Batman (Soundtrack – Prince)
9 songs from the smash hit soundtrack, including the hit
"Batdance."
___00290227 ....$5.95

93. Songs Of The 80's – The Decade Series
30 top hits, including: Careless Whisper • Don't Worry, Be
Happy • Ebony And Ivory • Endless Love • Every Breath You
Take • Fast Car • Hard Habit To Break • Islands In The
Stream • Kokomo • Lost In Your Eyes • Memory • I'll Be
Loving You (Forever) • We Didn't Start The Fire • Sailing •
Sara • Soldier Of Love These Dreams • Total Eclipse Of The
Heart • What's Love Got To Do With It • With Or Without You.
___00290241 ....$12.95

194. New Kids On The Block – Hangin' Tough
10 songs from these teen sensations, including: Please
Don't Go Girl • I'll Be Loving You (Forever) • Hangin'
Tough • (You've Got It) The Right Stuff • Cover Girl.
___00290238 ....$5.95

195. A Treasury Of Songs
70 big favorites, including: American Pie • Do You Know
the Way To San Jose • Eye In The Sky • I Write The Songs
• Imagine • It's Still Rock & Roll To Me • Just The Way
You Are • Longer • A Night In Tunisia • Sailing • San
Francisco • Walk On By • and many more.
___00290266 ....$15.95

196. Top Country Favorites
20 of country's favorites, including: All The Gold In
California • Forever And Ever, Amen • God Bless The
U.S.A. • Kiss You All Over • Lookin' For Love • Me And
Bobby McGee • Thank God And Greyhound.
___00290265 ....$5.95

197. Metal Rock Hits
18 classic hard rock singles, including: Angel • Foxey
Lady • I Hate Myself For Loving You • Livin' On A Prayer
• Pour Some Sugar On Me • Round And Round.
___00290133 ....$5.95

198. Ricky Van Shelton Songbook
14 songs from this country superstar, featuring: Don't We All
Have The Right • From A Jack To A King • I'll Leave This
World Loving You • Life Turned Her That Way • Living Proof.
___00290134 ....$6.95

199. Big Book Of Children's Songs
89 songs that children know and love, including: America,
The Beautiful • Bingo • Goober Peas • He's Got The
Whole World In His Hands • John Jacob Jingleheimer
Schmidt • Twinkle, Twinkle, Little Star • and more.
___00290169 ....$9.95

200. Frank Sinatra Songbook
92 songs recorded by Sinatra, including: All The Way • The
Birth Of The Blues • High Hopes • The Lady Is A Tramp •
Love And Marriage • Nancy (With The Laughing Face) •
Theme From New York, New York • Night And Day • Summer
Wind • Time After Time • Witchcraft • Young At Heart.
___00290119 ....$17.95

201. The Masters – Bach
36 melodies, including: Air For The G String • Fugue In G
Minor ("Little") • Jesu, Joy Of Man's Desiring • My Heart
Ever Faithful • Toccata And Fugue In D Minor: Toccata.
___00290221 ....$5.95

202. The Masters – Beethoven
34 melodies, including: Fur Elise • Piano Sonata No. 14
("Moonlight") (1st Movement) • Symphony No. 5 (1st
Movement) • Symphony No. 9 (4th Movement) ("Ode To
Joy") • Turkish March (From "The Ruins Of Athens").
___00290222 ....$5.95

203. The Masters – Brahms
29 melodies, including: Academic Festival Overture •
Hungarian Dance No. 5 • Lullaby • Symphony No. 1 (1st
Movement) • Waltz, Op. 39, No. 15.
___00290229 ....$5.95

204. The Masters – Chopin
31 songs, including: Etude, op. 10, No. 12 ("Revolutionary") • Fantaisie-Impromptu • Nocturne, Op. 9, No. 2 • Polonaise, Op. 40, No. 1 ("Military") • Waltz, Op. 64, No. 1 ("Minute").
_____ 00290230..$5.95

205. The Masters – Handel
34 songs, including: Hallelujah Chorus (From "Messiah") • The Harmonious Blacksmith • Largo (From "Xerxes") • See, The Conquering Hero Comes! (From "Judas Maccabeus") • Where'er You Walk (From "Semele").
_____ 00290231..$5.95

206. The Masters – Mozart
32 melodies, including: Eine Kleine Nachtmusik (1st Movement) • La Ci Darem La Mano (From "Don Giovanni") • Piano Sonata In C (1st Movement) • Symphony No. 40 (1st Movement) • Variations On "Twinkle, Twinkle Little Star".
_____ 00290223..$5.95

207. The Masters – Schubert
34 melodies, including: Ave Maria • The Erl King (Erlkonig) • Marche Militaaire • Moment Musical No. 3 • Symphony No. 8 ("Unfinished") (1st Movement).
_____ 00290232..$5.95

208. The Masters – Strauss
19 melodies, including: By The Beautiful Blue Danube • Emperor Waltzes • My Dear Marquis • Pizzicato Polka • Tales From The Vienna Woods.
_____ 00290234..$5.95

209. The Masters – Tchaikovsky
32 melodies, including: 1812 Overture • Piano Concerto No. 1 (1st Movement) • Romeo And Juliet • Sleeping Beauty Waltz.
_____ 00290224..$5.95

210. The Little Mermaid
The matching folio to this hit Disney movie. Features color photos and 8 songs including the Oscar-winning "Under The Sea." Also: Daughters Of Triton • Kiss The Girl • Fathoms Below • more.
_____ 00244110..$7.95

211. Chart Picks
18 big chart hits, including: How Am I Supposed To Live Without You • All Around The World • Hold On • Black Velvet • We Didn't Start The Fire • and more.
_____ 00244111..$6.95

212. Teenage Mutant Ninja Turtles
8 radical turtle tunes from the movie sensation, including: T-U-R-T-L-E Power • Spin That Wheel • Every Heart Needs A Home • Turtle Rhapsody • more! Also features 16 pages of color photos of your favorite heroes.
_____ 00244112..$7.95

213. The Phantom Of The Opera
9 songs from this Broadway smash, including: All I Ask Of You • The Point Of No Return • The Phantom Of The Opera • and more.
_____ 00244117..$8.95

214. Best Of Aerosmith
18 of their best, including: Back In the Saddle • Dude (Looks Like A Lady) • Sweet Emotion • Walk This Way • Love In An Elevator • Janie's Got a Gun • What It Takes.
_____ 00244116..$8.95

215. Best Of Patsy Cline
24 great songs, including: Crazy • I Fall To Pieces • San Antonio Rose • Three Cigarettes In An Ashtray • Your Cheatin' Heart • Why Can't He Be You • and more.
_____ 00244118..$5.9

216. Hot Pops
25 chartbusters from today's biggest stars, including: Another Day In Paradise • The End Of The Innocence • Escapade • If I Could Turn Back Time • The Living Years • Nothing Compares 2U • Vogue • and more!
_____ 00244119..$8.9

217. New Kids On The Block – Step By Step
10 songs from the latest release of this superstar group, including: Step By Step • Tonight • Games • Happy Birthday • and more.
_____ 00244123..$6.9

218. Sandi Patti Anthology
39 of her best, complete with a biography and lots of photos. Songs include: How Majestic Is Your Name • It's Your Song Lord • Let There Be Praise • Love In Any Language • Make His Praise Glorious • More Than Wonderful • O Magnify The Lord • and more.
_____ 00244124..$14.9

219. Hits Of The Ragtime Era
21 ragtime favorites, including: Alexander's Ragtime Band • Maple Leaf Rag • That's A Plenty • 12th Street Rag and many more.
_____ 00244138..$5.9

220. Wilson Phillips
Matching folio to their smash debut, featuring: Hold On • Impulsive • Release Me • and 7 more.
_____ 00244139..$6.9

221. Bad English
13 songs from this superstar collaboration debut, including: Heaven Is A 4-Letter Word • Possession • Price Of Love • When I See You Smile • and more.
_____ 00244140..$6.9

222. Movie Songs Of The 80's
25 movie hits including: Against All Odds (Take A Look At Me Now) • Almost Paradise • Footloose • Ghostbusters • The Greatest Love Of All • I Just Called To Say I Love You • Take My Breath Away • (I've Had) The Time Of My Life • and more.
_____ 00244141..$7.9

223. 55 Super Standards
55 all-time favorites, including: Blue Moon • Don't Make My Brown Eyes Blue • Hey Look Me Over • Isn't It Romantic • It Don't Mean A Thing (If It Ain't Got That Swing) • Mona Lisa • Over The Rainbow • Singin' In The Rain • That's Amore • You Are So Beautiful • and more.
_____ 00244142..$10.9

224. 56 Super Standards
56 more favorites, including: Blue Hawaii • Georgia On My Mind • I'm In The Mood For Love • Moon River • Nobody Does It Better • Shadow Of Your Smile • Tennesse Waltz • Theme From New York, New York • Up Where We Belong • We've Only Just Begun • and more.
_____ 00244143..$10.9

25. 57 Super Standards
7 classics, including: Buttons And Bows • Chattanooga Choo Choo • The Great Pretender • Moonglow • Talk To The Animals • A Time For Us • Volare • and more.
___00244144 ....$10.95

26. Great Love Songs
6 sentimental favorites, featuring: For Once In My Life • The Greatest Gift Of All • I Honestly Love You • I Just Called To Say I Love You • Love Story • Up Where We Belong • You Are So Beautiful • You Light Up My Life.
___00244145 ....$6.95

27. 18 Of The 80's Greatest Hits
18 big hits, including: Almost Paradise • Back In The High Life Again • Forever Your Girl • Hungry Eyes • Up Where We Belong • and more.
___00244146 ....$5.95

28. 22 More Greatest Hits Of The 80's
22 of the decade's best, including: Fame • The Greatest Love Of All • The Lady In Red • Straight Up • Take My Breath Away • Walk Like An Egyptian • and more.
___00244147 ....$6.95

29. Madonna – I'm Breathless
12 songs from and inspired by the film *Dick Tracy*, including: Vogue • Sooner Or Later • What Can You Lose? • Cry Baby • and more.
___00244148 ....$7.95

30. Willie Nelson Greatest Hits
18 classics from this country music legend, featuring: Always On My Mind • Blue Eyes Crying In The Rain • Crazy • Help Me Make It Through The Night • Make The World Go Away • Mammas Don't Let Your Babies Grow Up To Be Cowboys • To All The Girls I've Loved Before • and many more.
___00244149 ....$7.95

31. Best Of Carpenters
12 of their very best, including: (They Long To Be) Close To You • Please Mr. Postman • Sing • Top Of The World • We've Only Just Begun • and more.
___00244150 ....$7.95

32. Jimi Hendrix – Smash Hits
13 Hendrix classics, including: All Along The Watchtower • Foxey Lady • Hey Joe • Purple Haze • The Wind Cries Mary • and more.
___00244151 ....$6.95

33. Best Of Gloria Estefan & Miami Sound Machine
17 of their best, including: Bad Boy • Don't Wanna Lose You • Falling In Love (Uh-Oh) •1-2-3 • Rhythm Is Gonna Get You • Words Get In The Way • and more.
___00244152 ....$6.95

34. Heart
9 great rock/pop hits, including: All I Wanna Do Is Make Love To You • Barracuda • Magic Man • Never • Nothin' At All • Dog And Butterfly • and more.
___00244153 ....$7.95

35. Paula Abdul – Forever Your Girl
10 songs from the smash debut album, including: Cold-hearted • Forever Your Girl • Opposites Attract • Straight Up • (It's Just) The Way That You Love Me • and more.
___00243001 ....$5.95

236. The Platters Anthology
19 R&B classics, including: Only You (And You Alone) • Smoke Gets In Your Eyes • (You've Got) The Magic Touch • The Great Pretender • and more.
___00243002 ....$6.95

237. Bon Jovi
16 of their best, including: Bad Medicine • Living In Sin • Livin' On A Prayer • Wanted Dead Or Alive • You Give Love A Bad Name • and more.
___00243003 ....$7.95

238. The Best Of Irving Berlin
28 all-time favorites, including: Always • Blue Skies • Easter Parade • God Bless America • Happy Holiday • Puttin' On The Ritz • There's No Business Like Show Business • White Christmas • and more.
___00243004 ....$6.95

239. #1 Songs Of The 80's
46 hits that went straight to the top, including: Addicted To Love • Careless Whisper • Don't Worry, Be Happy • Every Breath You Take • Flashdance...What A Feeling • I Love Rock 'N Roll • Physical • Sailing • Total Eclipse Of The Heart • We Didn't Start The Fire • and many more!
___00243005 ....$12.95

240. Mariah Carey
Matching folio to her smash hit debut album, featuring 11 songs: Vision Of Love • I Don't Wanna Cry • Someday • Love Takes Time • and more.
___00243006 ....$7.95

241. Let's Play Nintendo Hits
A fun songbook with over 20 familiar tunes and lots of your favorite Nintendo characters. Includes themes from Dr. Mario, Legend Of Zelda, Rad Racer, Super Mario Bros., and more.
___00243007 ....$6.95

242. Love Takes Time & 12 Other Hits Of The 90's
13 songs, including the number one hits: Black Cat • I Don't Have The Heart • Love Takes Time • Praying For Time • Vision Of Love • and more.
___00243008 ....$5.95

243. The Greatest American Songbook
A 37-song salute to American heart-warmers, such as: America, The Beautiful • The Eagle • From A Distance • God Bless The U.S.A. • Imagine • The Star Spangled Banner • Stars And Stripes Forever • The Yankee Doodle Boy • and more.
___00243009 ....$7.95

244. Roy Orbison – Classic Hits
25 of his best, including the 1991 Grammy Award winning song "Oh, Pretty Woman" and: Crying • You Got It • Working For The Man • Blue Angel • Dream Baby (How Long Must I Dream) • and more.
___00243014 ....$8.95

245. The Simpsons™ Sing The Blues
Matching folio to the debut album by one of the most popular families on television. 11 songs made famous by Bart and the rest of the gang, including: Do The Bartman • Deep, Deep Trouble • Theme from "The Simpsons" • and more.
___00243016 ....$6.95

246. Basia – Best Of Two Albums: *Time And Tide* And *London Warsaw New York*
20 songs from these two best-selling albums. Includes: New Day For You • Promises • Time And Tide • Cruising For Bruising.
____00243017 ....$8.95

247. Michael Bolton – Soul Provider
All 10 songs from the chart-topping album plus 2 bonus tracks from The Hunger, including the songs: How Am I Supposed To Live Without You • How Can We Be Lovers • From Now On • Georgia On My Mind • and more.
____00243018 ....$5.95

248. John Lennon – Imagine
Matching folio to the soundtrack from this Lennon documentary. 20 songs, including: The Ballad Of John and Yoko • Give Peace A Chance • Imagine • Revolution • Stand By Me • (Just Like) Starting Over • Woman • and more.
____00243024 ....$6.95

249. The Best Of Steve Winwood
16 of his best, including: Back In The High Life Again • Don't You Know What The Night Can Do? • The Finer Things • Gimme Some Lovin' • Higher Love • Roll With It • Valerie • While You See A Chance • and more.
____00243082 ....$6.95

250. Smash Hits Of The 90's
22 of the decade's best, including: Baby Baby • Emotions • (Everything I Do) I Do It For You • More Than Words • Rush Rush • Someday • Unbelievable • and more.
____00243080 ....$8.95

251. Michael W. Smith – Go West Young Man
Matching folio to his latest album, featuring 10 songs: Place In This World • For You • Go West Young Man • plus photos and 3 bonus songs from his previous albums.
____00243085 ....$5.95

252. George Harrison Anthology
28 of his best, including: All Those Years Ago • Give Me Love (Give Me Peace On Earth) • Got My Mind Set On You • Here Comes the Sun • My Sweet Lord • When We Was Fab • While My Guitar Gently Weeps • and more.
____00243079 ....$8.95

256. Beauty And The Beast
8 songs from Disney's classic complete with beautiful full-color art throughout. Songs include: Beauty And The Beast • Belle • Be Our Guest • and more.
____00243081 ....$8.95

257. The Best Of The Doobie Brothers
15 of their classics, including: China Grove • The Doctor • Jesus Is Just Alright • Listen To The Music • Minute By Minute • Takin' It To The Streets • What A Fool Believes • and more.
____00243086 ....$6.95

258. The Best Of Fleetwood Mac
20 of their timeless hits, including: Go Your Own Way • Hold Me • Little Lies • Rhiannon • Sara • Tusk • You Make Loving Fun • and more.
____00243083 ....$6.95

259. Dwight Yoakam – Greatest Hits
13 songs from this country superstar: Guitars, Cadillacs • Honky Tonk Man • Little Sister • Little Ways • Streets of Bakersfield.
____00243084 ....$5.95

260. Billboard Songbook Series – Composite 1955-195⬭
Five books – 80 songs! – conveniently bound in on⬭ edition. Includes: Unchained Melody • Hound Dog • Blueberry Hill • At The Hop • Personality • and more.
____00290012 ....$17.9⬭

261. Billboard Songbook Series – Composite 1960-196⬭
Five books in one! Over 70 songs, including: It's Now O⬭ Never • Hit The Road Jack • Return To Sender • It's M⬭ Party • I Want To Hold Your Hand • and more.
____00290018 ....$17.9⬭

262. Billboard Songbook Series – Composite 1965-196⬭
86 classic hits, including: Turn! Turn! Turn! • Wild Thin⬭ • Daydream Believer • Born To Be Wild • Hey Jude • Suspicious Minds • and more.
____00290024 ....$17.9⬭

263. Billboard Songbook Series – Composite 1970-197⬭
Five books – 84 songs – in one compilation. Includes: L⬭ It Be • Maggie May • American Pie • You're So Vain • Band On The Run • Bennie And The Jets • and more.
____00290030 ....$17.9⬭

267. The Best Of Reba McEntire
A perfect souvenir collection of 21 of Reba's favorit⬭ songs. Song highlights include: Only In My Mind • Somebody Should Leave • What Am I Gonna Do About Yo⬭ • Whoever's In New England • Sunday Kind Of Love • Yo⬭ Lie • and more.
____00243088 ....$7.9⬭

268. Garth Brooks – No Fences
Matching folio to the hit album with 10 songs. Includes Friends In Low Places • The Thunder Rolls • Two Of ⬭ Kind, Workin' On A Full House • Unanswered Prayers • Wild Horses.
____00243106 ....$5.9⬭

269. Garth Brooks – Ropin' The Wind
All 10 songs from this #1 blockbuster featuring: Shameles⬭ • Papa Loved Mama • Rodeo • What She's Doing Now • and more.
____00243109 ....$5.9⬭

270. Billboard Top Country Songs Of The 60's
A great compilation of 62 songs and background text o⬭ this whole era of country music. Includes: Act Naturally • Crazy • D-I-V-O-R-C-E • Daddy Sang Bass • Green Gree⬭ Grass Of Home • King Of The Road • Make The World G⬭ Away • Okie From Muskogee • Ruby, Don't Take You⬭ Love To Town • She's Got You • and more.
____00243110 ....$12.9⬭

271. Billboard Top Country Songs Of The 70's
62 songs complete with text for this era in country musi⬭ Songs include: Come On In • Daydreams About Nigh⬭ Things • Every Which Way But Loose • The Gambler • Help Me Make It Through The Night • (Hey Won't Yo⬭ Play) Another Somebody Done Somebody Wrong Song • I'm Not Lisa • Luckenbach, Texas • Mammas Don't Le⬭ Your Babies Grow Up To Be Cowboys • and more.
____00243111 ....$12.9⬭

272. Billboard Top Country Songs Of The 80's
54 songs and text from the decade's biggest country stars. Includes: Coward Of The County • Forever And Ever, Amen • God Bless The U.S.A. • I Was Country When Country Wasn't Cool • I Wouldn't Have Missed It For The World • Islands In The Stream • and more.
____00243112 ....$12.95

273. Billboard Top Rock 'n' Roll Hits of the '60s
61 hits that made this decade so memorable, including: Born To Be Wild • Duke Of Earl • Gloria • Good Lovin' • Hey Jude • I Can See For Miles • It's My Party • The Lion Sleeps Tonight • Louie Louie • Monday, Monday • People Got To Be Free • Stand By Me • The Twist • Under The Boardwalk • White Room • Wooly Bully • and more.
____00243156 ....$12.95

274. Billboard Top Rock 'n' Roll Hits of the '70s
50 of the decade's biggest hits, including: All Right Now • Band On The Run • Bennie And The Jets • Brandy (You're A Fine Girl) • Crocodile Rock • Free Bird • Goodbye Yellow Brick Road • I Will Survive • I'm Just A Singer In A Rock 'N Roll Band • I've Got The Music In Me • Jesus Is Just All Right With Me • Knock Three Times • Let It Be • Maggie May • Me And Bobby McGee • Midnight Train To Georgia • My Sweet Lord • Night Fever • Philadelphia Freedom • Reelin' In The Years • She's Some Kind Of Wonderful • Silly Love Song • Takin' Care Of Business • We Just Disagree • and more.
____00243157 ....$12.95

275. Billboard Top Rock 'n' Roll Hits of the '80s
46 songs that topped the charts in the 80s, including: Addicted to Love • Every Breath You Take • Every Rose Has Its Thorn • Express Yourself • Faith • I Love Rock 'N Roll • I Want To Know What Love Is • Livin' On A Prayer • Straight Up • Total Eclipse Of The Heart • We Didn't Start The Fire • What's Love Got To Do With It • With Or Without You • and more.
____00243158 ....$12.95

276. The Best Of Buck Owens
Over 20 of his best, including: Act Naturally • Crying Time • I've Got A Tiger By The Tail • Love's Gonna Live Here • Open Up Your Heart • Waitin' In Your Welfare Line • and more.
____00243514 ....$6.95

277. The Best Of Rod Stewart
30 Stewart classics: Downtown Train • The First Cut Is The Deepest • Forever Young • Infatuation • Maggie May • Passion • Rhythm Of My Heart • This Old Heart Of Mine • Tonight's The Night • You're In My Heart • Young Turks • and more.
____00243507 ....$10.95

278. Nelson – After The Rain
The matching folio to their debut album. All 9 songs, including "After The Rain" and "(Can't Live Without Your) Love And Affection."
____00243508 ....$5.95

279. Classical Themes From The Movies
Over 25 pieces of well-known music from movies like 2001: A Space Odyssey, Ordinary People, Pretty Woman, Moonstruck, Fatal Attraction, Amadeus, and more! Pieces include: Also Sprach Zarathustra • Ave Maria • Blue Danube Waltz • The Minute Waltz • Toreador Song from Carmen • and more.
____00243509 ....$5.95

280. Broadway Musicals Show By Show – 1891-1916
33 classics with background text from shows such as: *Robin Hood, Babes In Toyland, The Merry Widow,* and more. Songs include: After The Ball • Give My Regards To Broadway • I Love You So! (The Merry Widow Waltz) • March Of The Toys • Mary's A Grand Old Name • Simple Melody • Streets Of New York • Toyland • and more.
____00243099 ....$8.95

281. Broadway Musicals Show By Show – 1917-1929
Over 40 songs from the era's most popular shows with interesting trivia about each, including: Can't Help Lovin' Dat Man • How Long Has This Been Going On? • Ol' Man River • A Pretty Girl Is Like A Melody • St. Louis Blues • Tea For Two • You Do Something To Me • You're The Cream In My Coffee • and more.
____00243100 ....$9.95

282. Broadway Musicals Show By Show – 1930-1939
A collection of over 45 songs and notes from the decade's biggest Broadway hits, includes: Begin The Beguine • Embraceable You • Falling In Love With Love • Friendship • I Get A Kick Out Of You • I Got Rhythm • The Lady Is A Tramp • My Funny Valentine • Smoke Gets In Your Eyes • Strike Up The Band • It Ain't Necessarily So • and more.
____00243101 ....$9.95

283. Broadway Musicals Show By Show – 1940-1949
Show descriptions by renowned Broadway historian Stanley Green and over 45 songs from Broadway hits including: Bali Hai • Bewitched • Diamond's Are A Girl's Best Friend • If I Loved You • New York, New York • Some Enchanted Evening • The Surrey With The Fringe On Top • You'll Never Walk Alone • more.
____00243102 ....$9.95

284. Broadway Musicals Show By Show – 1950-1959
55 songs from such classics as *The King And I, My Fair Lady, West Side Story, Gypsy, The Sound Of Music,* and more. Songs include: Edelweiss • Everything's Coming Up Roses • Getting To Know You • I've Grown Accustomed To Her Face • Mack The Knife • Maria • Shall We Dance? • Somewhere • and more.
____00243103 ....$9.95

285. Broadway Musicals Show By Show – 1960-1971
Over 45 songs from shows such as *Oliver!, Cabaret, Hello, Dolly!, Fiddler On The Roof, Jesus Christ Superstar, Mame,* and more. Songs include: As Long As He Needs Me • Consider Yourself • Day By Day • I Don't Know How To Love Him • If Ever I Would Leave You • If I Were A Rich Man • People • Sunrise, Sunset • and more.
____00243104 ....$9.95

286. Broadway Musicals Show By Show – 1972-1988
Over 30 songs from the era of big productions like *Phantom Of The Opera, Evita, La Cage Aux Folles, Les Miserables, Me And My Girl, A Chorus Line, Cats* and more. Songs include: All I Ask Of You • Don't Cry For Me Argentina • I Am What I Am • I Dreamed A Dream • Memory • The Music Of The Night • On My Own • Tomorrow • What I Did For Love • and more.
____00243105 ....$9.95

287. The Best Of Crosby, Stills & Nash
14 of their best, including: Marrakesh Express • Southern Cross • Wasted On The Way • and more.
____00243510..$5.95

289. The Best Of Randy Travis
11 songs, including: Deeper Than The Holler • A Few Ole Country Boys • It's Just A Matter Of Time • Point Of Light • and more.
____00243512..$5.95

290. The Travis Tritt Songbook
18 songs, including: Drift Off To Dream • Help Me Hold On • Here's A Quarter (Call Someone Who Cares) • Put Some Drive In Your Country • and more.
____00243089..$7.95

291. The Mamas And The Papas – 16 Of Their Greatest Hits
16 of their best, including: California Dreamin' • Dedicated To The One I Love • I Saw Her Again Last Night • Monday, Monday • and more.
____00243506..$5.95

292. Mariah Carey – Emotions
Matching folio to her second album featuring 10 songs, including the hit singles Emotions • Can't Let Go • Make It Happen • and more.
____00243513..$6.95

293. Kenny Loggins Greatest Hits
17 songs, including: Danger Zone • Footloose • I'm Alright • This Is It • What A Fool Believes • and more.
____00243115..$7.95

294. The Best Of John Mellencamp
16 songs, including: Authority Song • Crumblin' Down • Hurts So Good • Lonely Ol' Night • Pink Houses • Rain On The Scarecrow • This Time • and more.
____00243126..$6.95

295. Christmas Songs For Kids
Over 25 songs kids love to hear, including: All I Want For Christmas Is My Two Front Teeth • The Chipmunk Song • Frosty The Snow Man • Jingle, Jingle, Jingle • Rudolph, The Red-Nosed Reindeer • Suzy Snowflake • more.
____00243114..$5.95

296. Country Superstars of the '90s
29 hot hits, including: Friends In Low Places (Garth Brooks) • Help Me Hold On (Travis Tritt) • Love Can Build A Bridge (The Judds) • Point Of Light (Randy Travis) • You Know Me Better Than That (George Strait) • You Lie (Reba McEntire) • and more.
____00243121..$8.95

297. Big Book Of Christmas Songs
A comprehensive collection of 125 songs, including: Angels We Have Heard On High • Auld Lang Syne • Away In A Manger • Deck The Hall • Hallelujah Chorus • I Heard The Bells On Christmas Day • Jingle Bells • Joy To The World • O Holy Night • Silent Night • The Twelve Days Of Christmas • Up On The Housetop • What Child Is This? • and more!
____00243122..$12.95

298. Michael Jackson – Dangerous
All 14 songs from the hit album, including: In The Closet • Remember The Time • Heal The World • Black Or White • and more.
____00243132..$8.95

299. Aladdin
All 8 pieces from Disney's latest blockbuster, complete with full color art. Songs include: A Whole New World • Friend Like Me • One Jump Ahead • and more.
____00243143..$7.95

401. "Emotions," "Can't Stop This Thing We Started" And Other Top Hits
14 chart-burners, including the title songs and: Cream • Everybody Plays The Fool • Something To Talk About • That's What Love Is For • When A Man Loves A Woman • and more.
____00243087..$5.95

402. "Don't Let The Sun Go Down On Me" And Other Top Recorded Hits
15 recent chart-topping hits, including: Can't Let Go • Get A Leg Up • Change • Set The Night To Music • and more.
____00243113..$5.95

403. "Tears In Heaven," "Good For Me" And Other Top Hits
13 of today's hottest hits, including the title songs and: Beauty And The Beast • Diamonds And Pearls • Mysterious Ways • Shameless • Smells Like Teen Spirit • and more.
____00243124..$5.95

Take this order form to your local music dealer or send directly to:

Hal Leonard Publishing Corporation

7777 West Bluemound Road P.O. Box 13819 Milwaukee, WI 53213

90500031

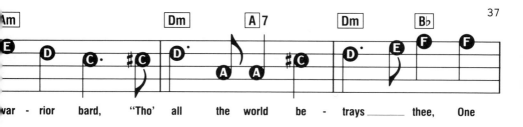

war - rior bard, "Tho' all the world be - trays————— thee, One

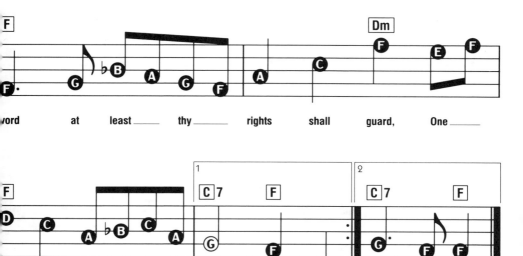

word at least————— thy————— rights shall guard, One—————

faith - ful heart————— shall praise thee!" The slav - er - y."

Additional Lyrics

2. The Minstrel fell,
   But the foe man's chain could not bring his proud soul under;
   The harp he loved ne'er spoke again,
   For he tore its chords asunder,
   And said, "No chain shall sully thee,
   Thou soul of love and bravery!
   Thy songs were made for the pure and free,
   They ne'er shall sound in slavery."

Molly Malone
(Cockles And Mussels)

Regi-Sound Program: 1
Rhythm: Waltz

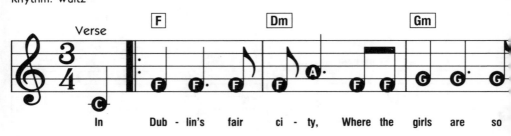

In Dub - lin's fair ci - ty, Where the girls are so

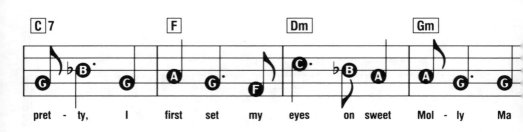

pret - ty, I first set my eyes on sweet Mol - ly Ma

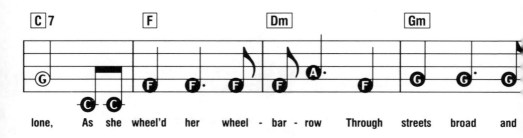

lone, As she wheel'd her wheel - bar - row Through streets broad and

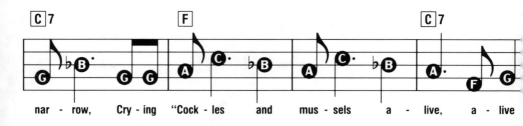

nar - row, Cry - ing "Cock - les and mus - sels a - live, a - live

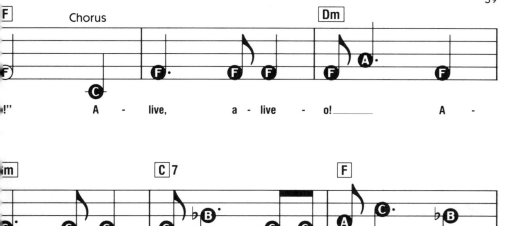

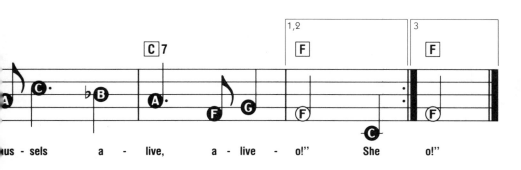

Additional Lyrics

2. She was a fishmonger, But sure 'twas no wonder,
   For so were her father and mother before,
   And they each wheel'd their barrow,
   Through streets broad and narrow,
   Crying "Cockles and mussels alive, alive-o!"
   CHORUS

3. She died of a fever, And no one could save her,
   And that was the end of sweet Molly Malone,
   But her ghost wheels her barrow
   Through streets broad and narrow,
   Crying "Cockles and mussels alive, alive-o!"
   CHORUS

My Wild Irish Rose

Regi-Sound Program: 2
Rhythm: Waltz

Words and Music by
Chauncey Olcott

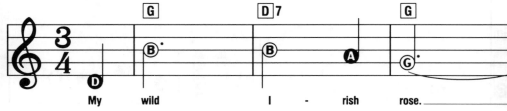

My wild I - rish rose. ___

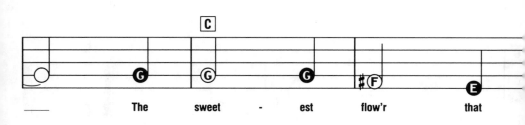

___ The sweet - est flow'r that

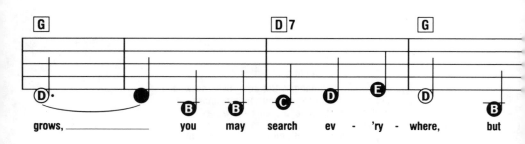

grows, ___ you may search ev - 'ry - where, but

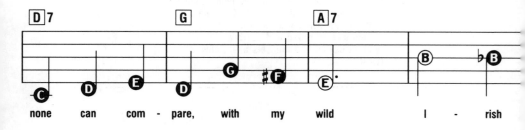

none can com - pare, with my wild I - rish

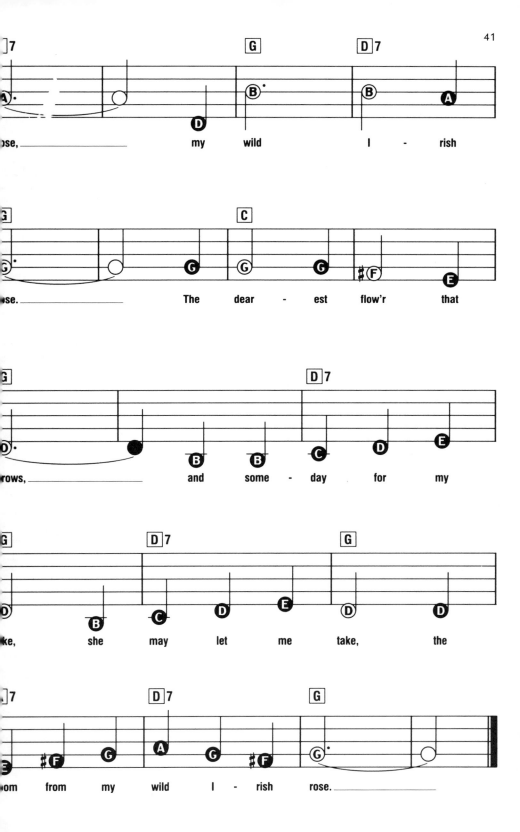

42

Mother Machree

Regi-Sound Program: 2
Rhythm: Waltz

Words by Rita Johnson Yo

Music by Ernest R. Ball and Chauncey Ol

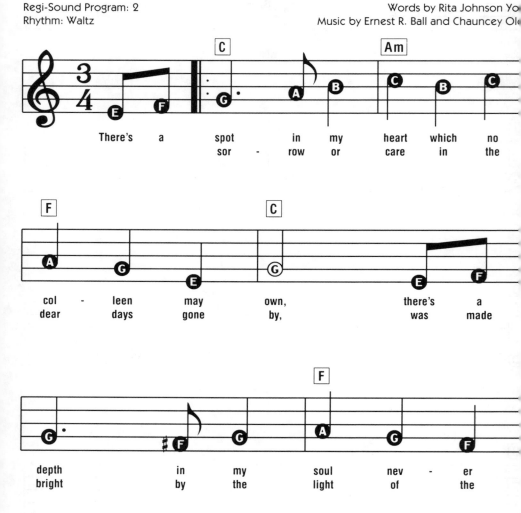

43

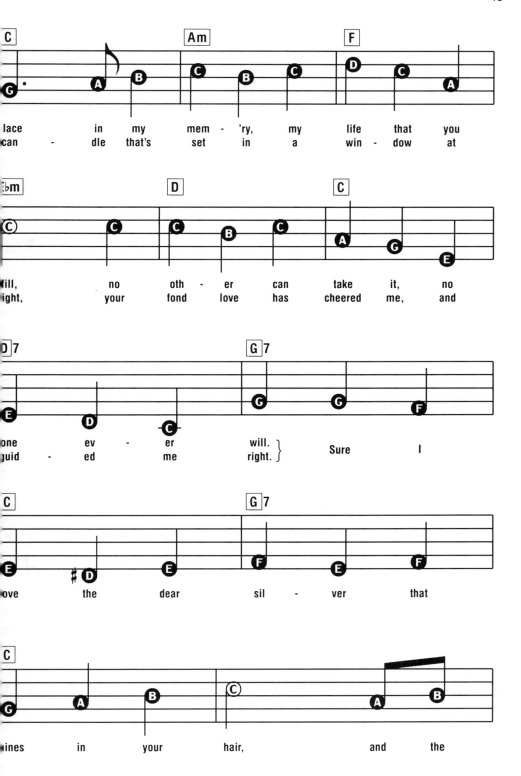

44

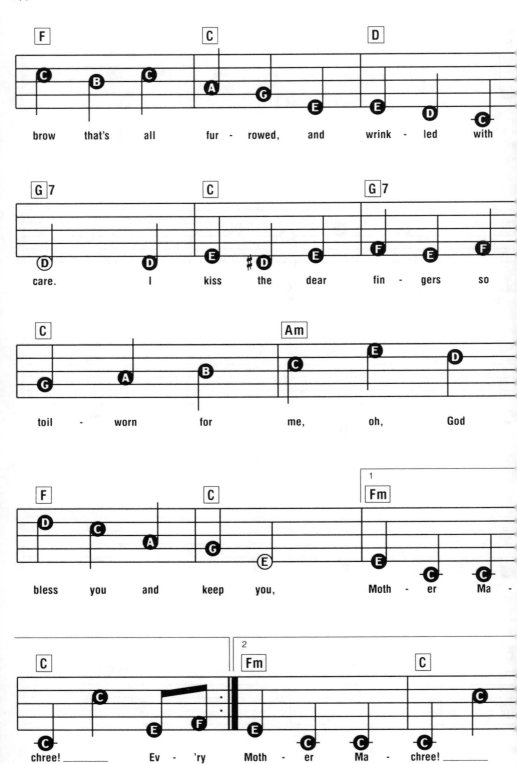

Rory O'Moore

i-Sound Program: 9
thm: 6/8 March

Young Ror-y O' Moore court-ed Kath-a-leen Bawn, he was
deed then," says Kath-leen, "don't think of the like for I
Kath-leen my dar-lint you've teas'd me e-nough, and I've

bold as a hawk, and she soft as the dawn. He
half gave a prom-ise to sooth-er-ing Mike. The
rash'd for your sake Din-ny Grimes and Jim Duff. And

ish'd in his heart pret-ty Kath-leen to please and he
'round that I walk on he loves, I'll be bound." "Faith," says
I've made myself drink-ing your health quite a beast, so I

ho't the best way to do that was to tease. "Now
Ror-y, "I'd rath-er love you than the ground." "Now
think af-ter that I may talk to the Priest." Then

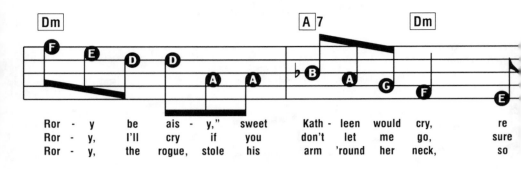

Ror -	y	be	ais -	y,"	sweet	Kath -	leen would	cry,	re
Ror -	y,	I'll	cry	if	you	don't	let me	go,	sure
Ror -	y,	the	rogue,	stole	his	arm	'round her	neck,	so

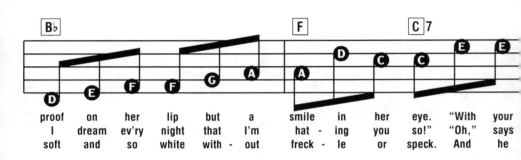

proof	on	her	lip	but	a	smile	in her	eye.	"With your
I	dream	ev'ry	night	that	I'm	hat -	ing you	so!"	"Oh," says
soft	and	so	white	with - out		freck -	le or	speck.	And he

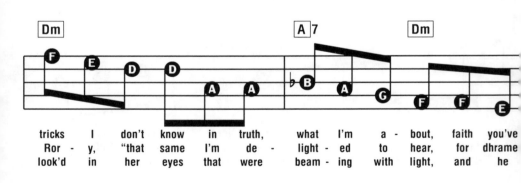

tricks	I	don't	know	in	truth,	what	I'm a -	bout,	faith you've
Ror -	y,	"that	same	I'm	de -	light -	ed to	hear,	for dhrame
look'd	in	her	eyes	that	were	beam -	ing with	light,	and he

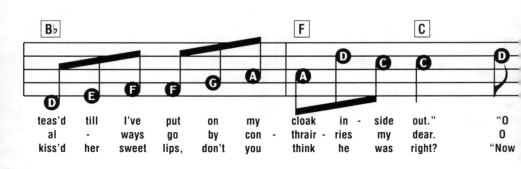

teas'd	till	I've	put	on	my	cloak	in - side	out."	"O
al -	ways	go	by	con -	thrair -	ies	my	dear.	O
kiss'd	her	sweet	lips,	don't	you	think	he was	right?	"Now

The Rose Of Tralee

Regi-Sound Program: 1
Rhythm: Waltz

Words and Music by Charles Glo
and C. Mordaunt Spen

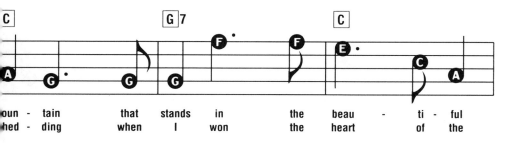

oun - tain   that   stands   in   the   beau - ti - ful
hed - ding   when   I   won   the   heart   of the

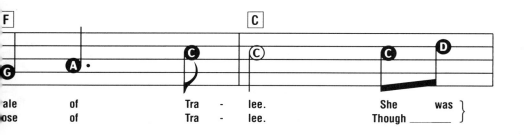

ale   of   Tra - lee.   She   was }
ose   of   Tra - lee.   Though _____ }

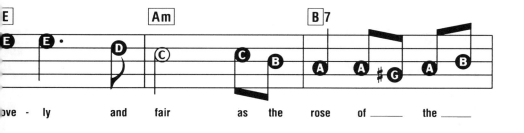

ove - ly   and   fair   as   the   rose   of ____ the ____

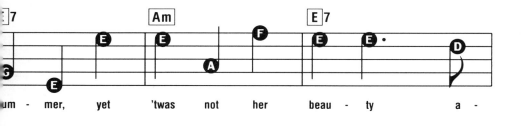

um - mer,   yet   'twas   not   her   beau - ty   a -

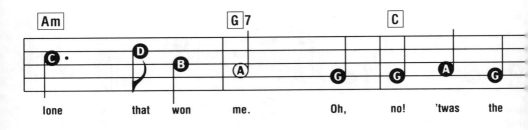

lone   that won   me.   Oh,   no!   'twas the

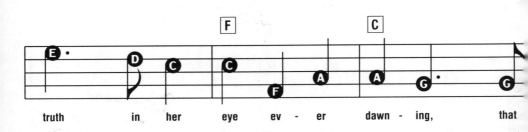

truth   in   her   eye   ev -   er   dawn - ing,   that

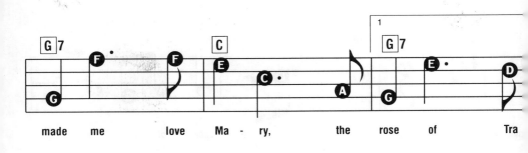

made   me   love   Ma - ry,   the   rose   of   Tra

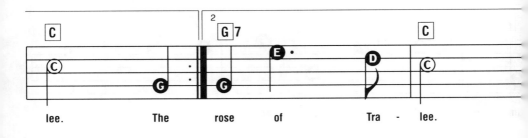

lee.   The   rose   of   Tra - lee.

The Wearing Of The Green

i-Sound Program: 9
thm: March or Polka

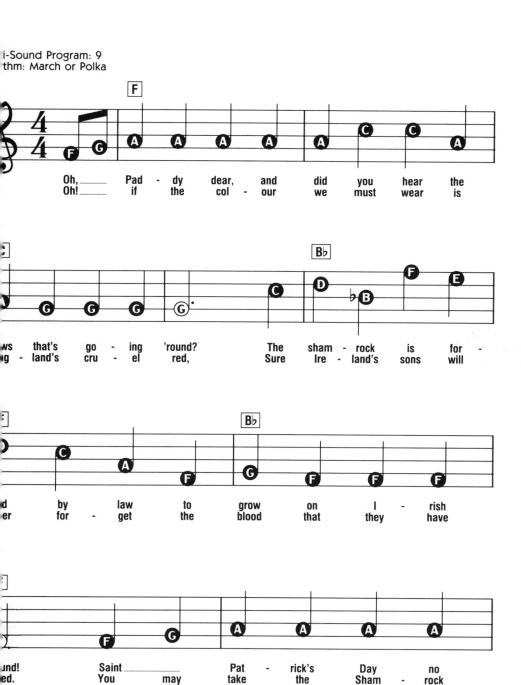

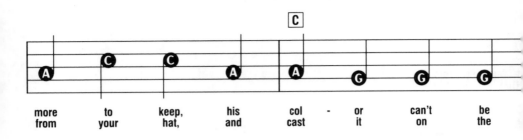

more to keep, his col - or can't be
from to your keep, hat, and cast it on the

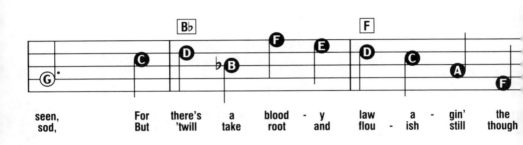

seen, For there's a blood - y law a - gin' the
sod, But 'twill take root and flou - ish still though

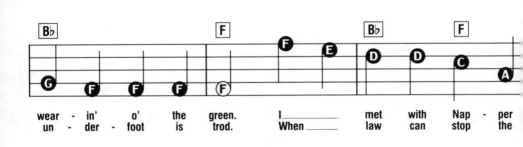

wear - in' o' the green. I____ met with Nap - per
un - der - foot is trod. When____ law can stop the

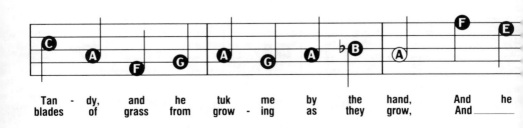

Tan - dy, and he tuk me by the hand, And he
blades of grass from grow - ing as they grow, And____

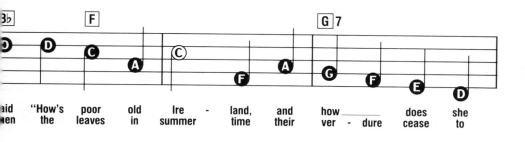

aid "How's poor old Ire - land, and how____ does she
en the leaves in summer time their ver - dure cease

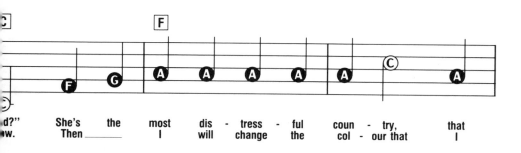

d?" She's the most dis - tress - ful coun - try, that
w. Then____ I will change the col - our that I

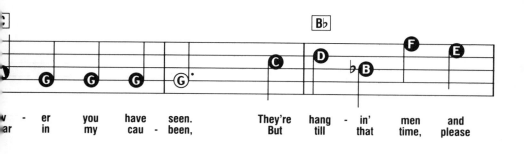

v - er you have seen. They're hang - in' men and
ar in my cau - been, But till that time, please

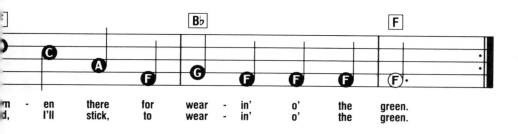

m - en there for wear - in' o' the green.
d, I'll stick, to wear - in' o' the green.

Sweet Rosie O'Grady

Regi-Sound Program: 4
Rhythm: Waltz

Words and Music
Maude Nug[

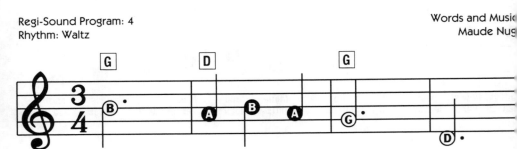

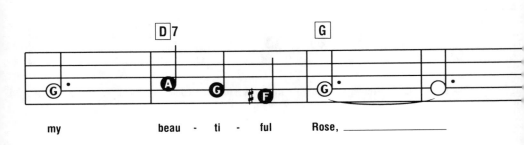

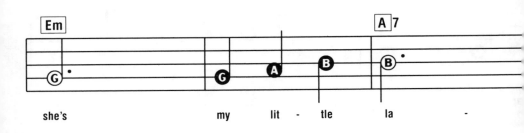

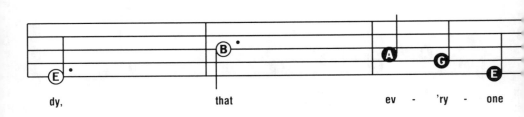

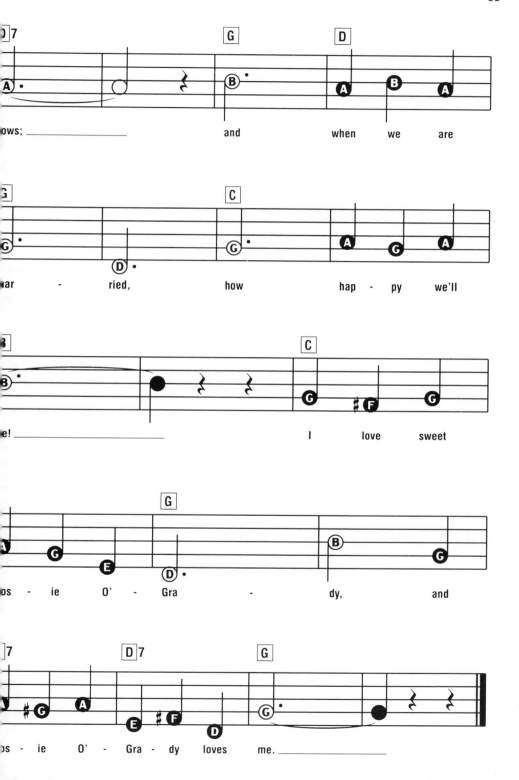

'Tis The Last Rose Of Summer

Regi-Sound Program: 10
Rhythm: Waltz

Words by Thomas Mo
Music by Richard Alfred Mill

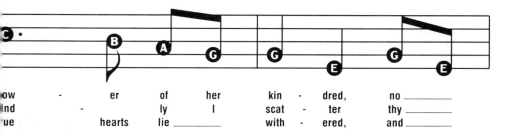

ow - er of her kin - dred, no _____
ind - ly I scat - ter thy _____
ue hearts lie _____ with - ered, and _____

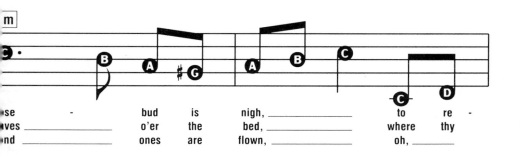

se - bud is nigh, _____ to re -
ves _____ o'er the bed, _____ where thy
nd _____ ones are flown, _____ oh, _____

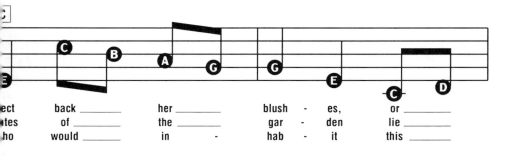

ect back _____ her _____ blush - es, or _____
tes of _____ the _____ gar - den lie _____
ho would _____ in - hab - it this _____

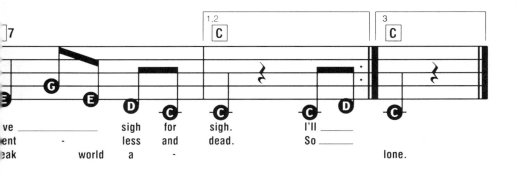

ve _____ sigh for sigh. I'll _____
ent - less and dead. So _____
eak world a - lone.

Too-Ra-Loo-Ra-Loo-Ral
(That's An Irish Lullaby)

Regi-Sound Program: 1
Rhythm: Waltz

Words and Mu
James R. Sha

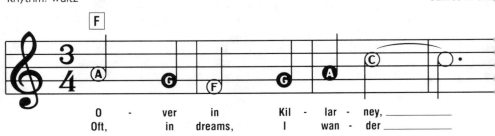

O - ver in Kil - lar - ney, _____
Oft, in dreams, I wan - der _____

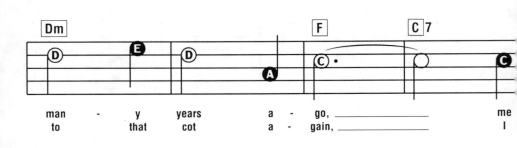

man - y years a - go, _____ me
to that cot years a - gain, _____ I

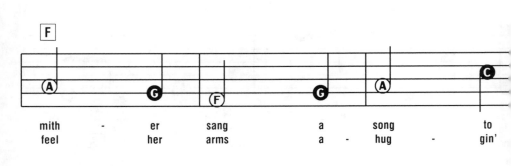

mith - er sang a song to
feel her arms a - hug - gin'

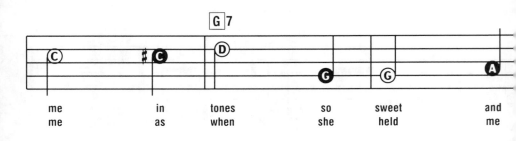

me in tones so sweet and
me as when she held me

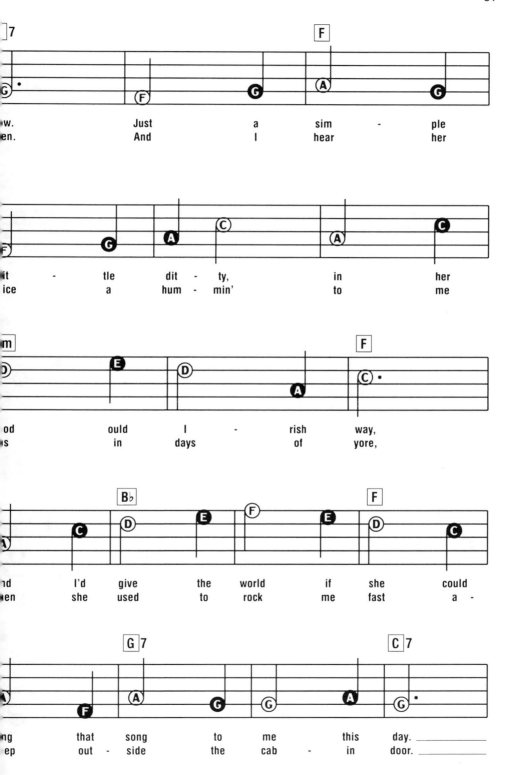

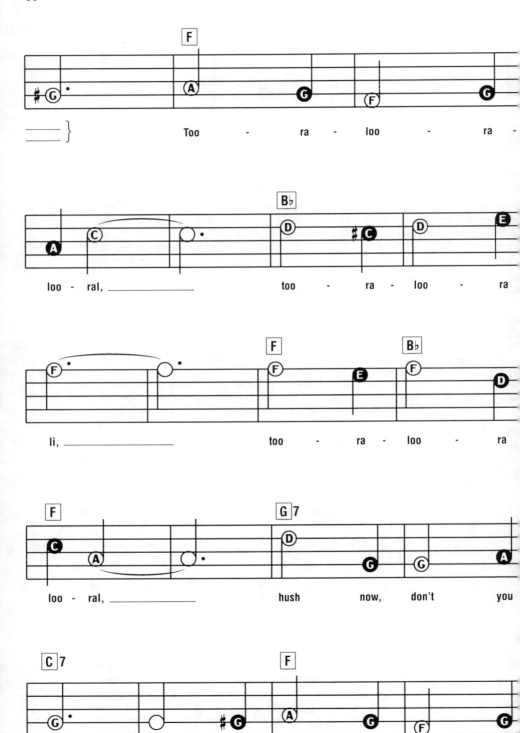

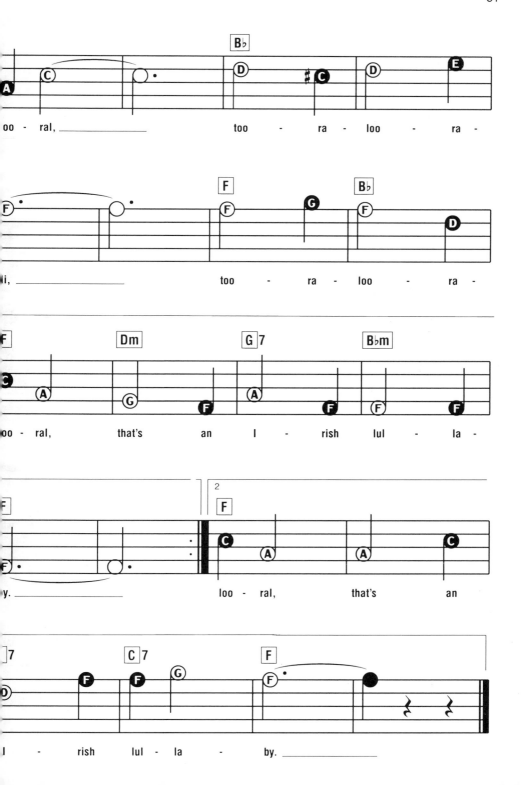

Tourelay

Regi-Sound Program: 8
Rhythm: Waltz

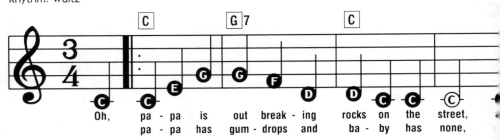

Oh, pa - pa is out break - ing rocks on the street,
pa - pa has gum - drops and ba - by has none,

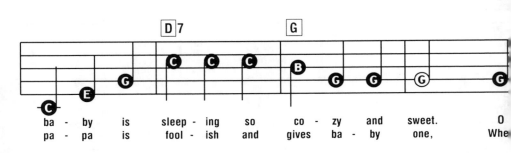

ba - by is sleep - ing so co - zy and sweet. O
pa - pa is fool - ish and gives ba - by one, Whe

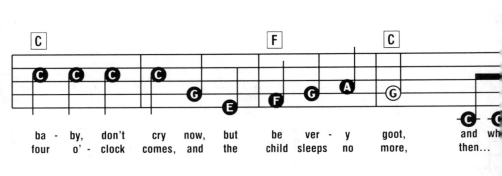

ba - by, don't cry now, but be ver - y goot, and wh
four o' - clock comes, and the child sleeps no more, then...

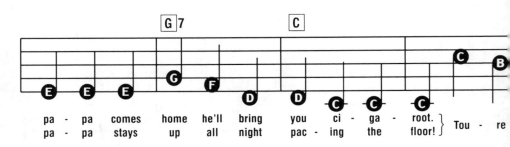

pa - pa comes home he'll bring you ci - ga - root. } Tou - re
pa - pa stays up all night pac - ing the floor!

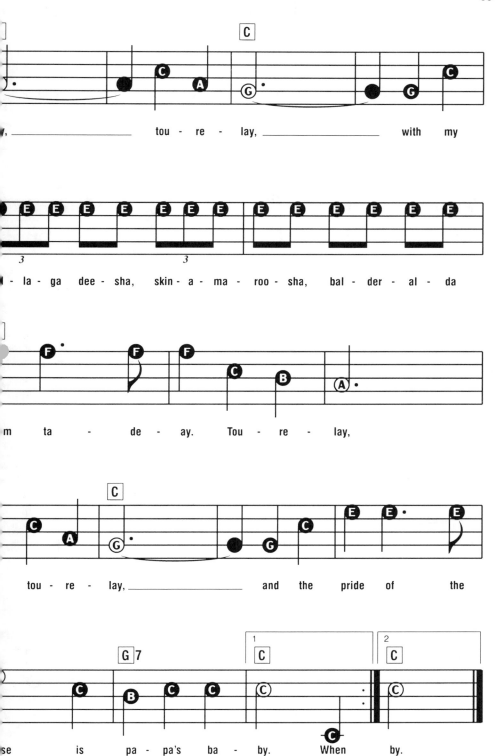

When Irish Eyes Are Smiling

Regi-Sound Program: 3
Rhythm: Waltz

Words by Chauncey Olcott and George Gra
Music by Ernest R

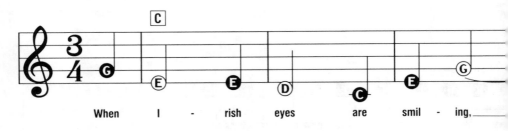

When I - rish eyes are smil - ing,____

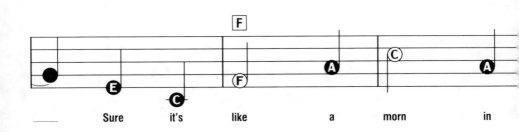

____ Sure it's like a morn in

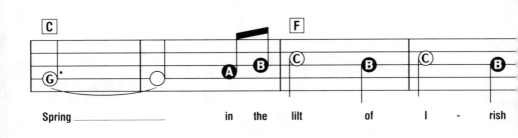

Spring ____ in the lilt of I - rish

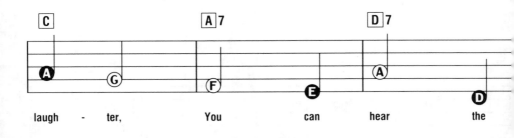

laugh - ter, You can hear the

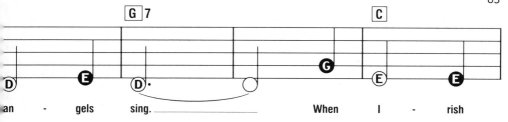

an - gels sing. When I - rish

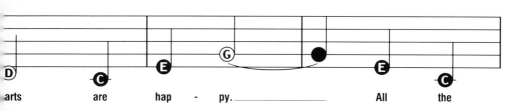

arts are hap - py. All the

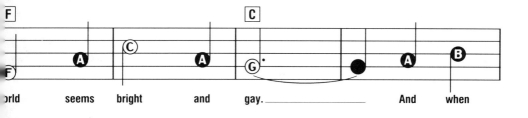

orld seems bright and gay. And when

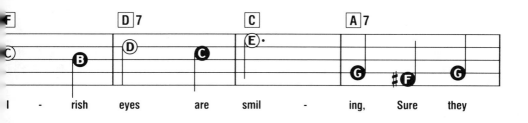

I - rish eyes are smil - ing, Sure they

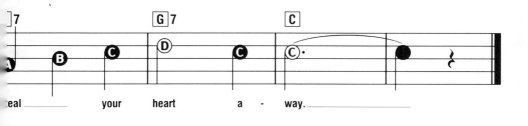

eal your heart a - way.

Where The River Shannon Flows

Regi-Sound Program: 10
Rhythm: 8 Beat or Pops

Words and Music
James J. Russ

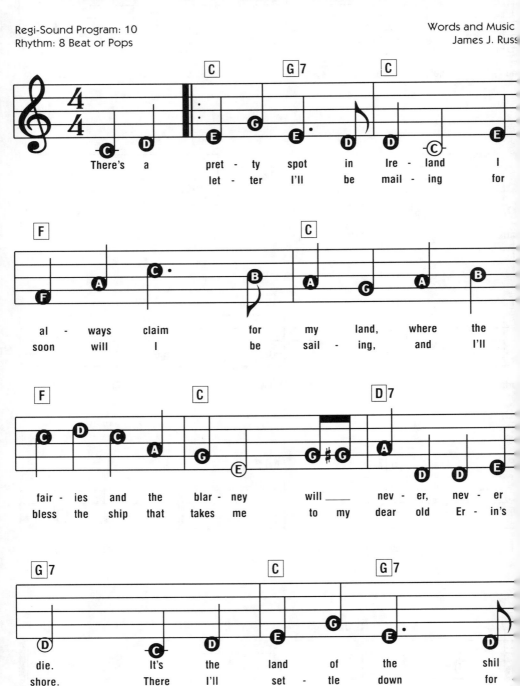

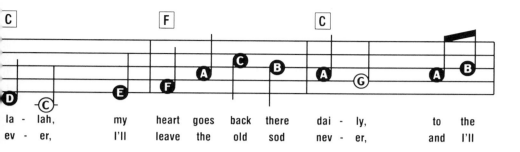

la - lah,   my   heart goes back there dai - ly,   to the
ev - er,   I'll   leave the old sod nev - er,   and I'll

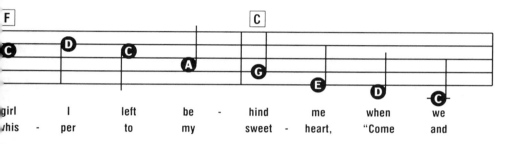

girl   I   left   be - hind   me   when   we
whis - per   to   my   sweet - heart,   "Come   and

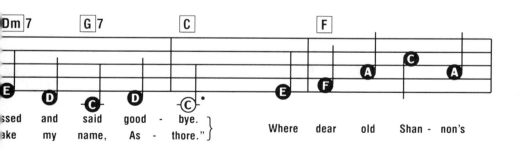

ssed   and   said   good - bye.   Where   dear   old   Shan - non's
ake   my   name,   As - thore."

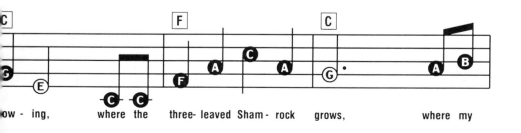

ow - ing,   where the   three- leaved Sham - rock   grows,   where my

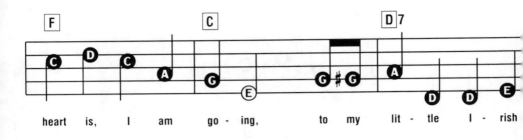

heart is, I am go - ing, to my lit - tle I - rish

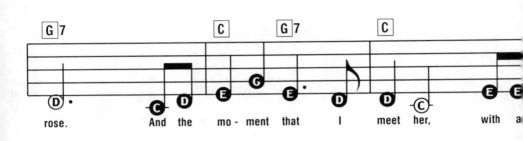

rose. And the mo - ment that I meet her, with a

hug and kiss I'll greet her, for there's not a col - leen

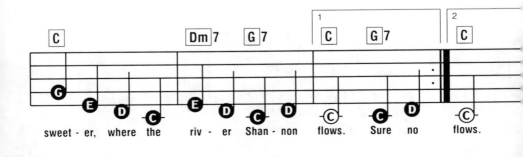

sweet - er, where the riv - er Shan - non flows. Sure no flows.

Who Threw The Overalls In Mistress Murphy's Chowder?

i-Sound Program: 7
thm: Rock or 8 Beat

Words and Music by
George L. Giefer

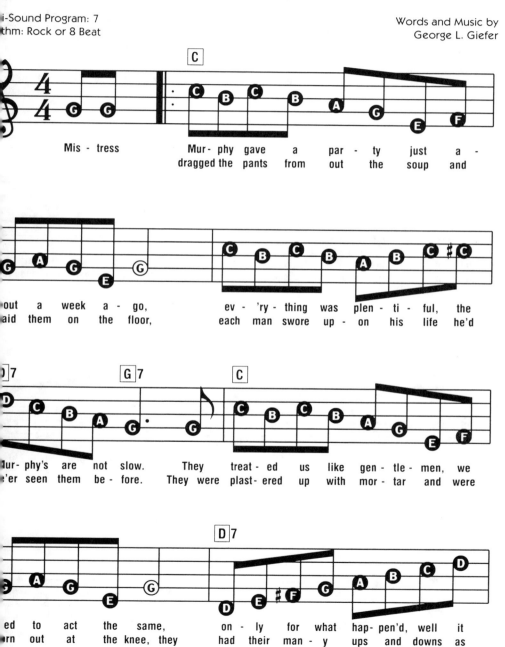

Mis - tress Mur - phy gave a par - ty just a -
dragged the pants from out the soup and

out a week a - go, ev - 'ry - thing was plen - ti - ful, the
aid them on the floor, each man swore up - on his life he'd

ur - phy's are not slow. They treat - ed us like gen - tle - men, we
er seen them be - fore. They were plast- ered up with mor - tar and were

ed to act the same, on - ly for what hap - pen'd, well it
rn out at the knee, they had their man - y ups and downs as

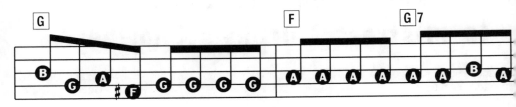

'twas an aw - ful shame, when Mis - tress Mur - phy dish'd the chow - der out she
we could plain - ly see, and when Mis - tress Mur - phy she came to she

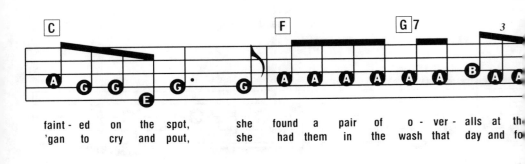

faint - ed on the spot, she found a pair of o - ver - alls at th
'gan to cry and pout, she had them in the wash that day and fo

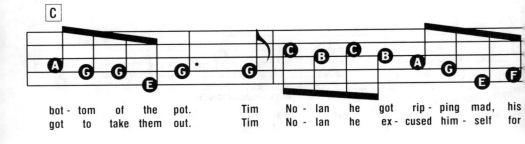

bot - tom of the pot. Tim No - lan he got rip - ping mad, his
got to take them out. Tim No - lan he ex - cused him - self for

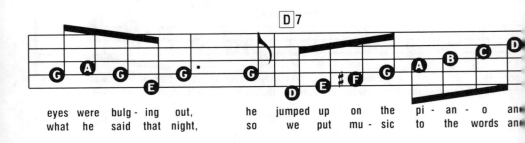

eyes were bulg - ing out, he jumped up on the pi - an - o an
what he said that night, so we put mu - sic to the words an

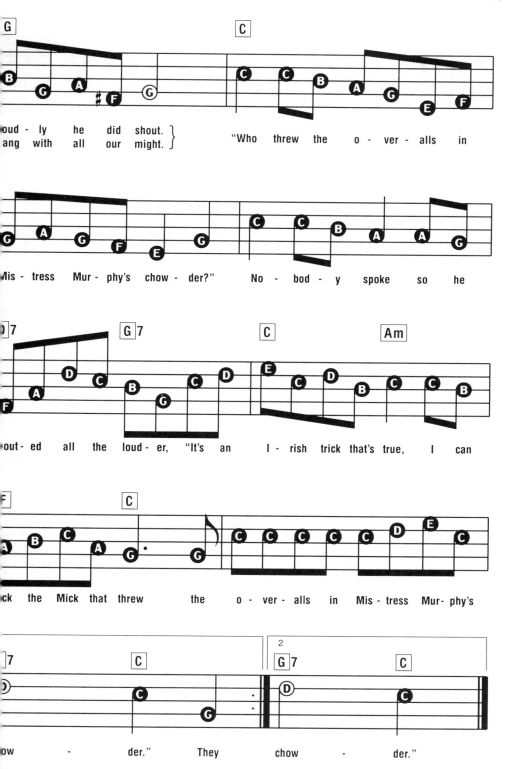

easy ELECTRONIC KEYBOARD MUSIC®

Regi-Sound Programs

- Match the Regi-Sound Program number on the song to the corresponding numbered category below. Select and activate an instrumental sound available on your instrument.
- Choose an automatic rhythm appropriate to the mood and style of the song. (Consult your Owner's Guide for proper operation of automatic rhythm features.)
- Adjust the tempo and volume controls to comfortable settings.

Regi-Sound
Program

1	Flute, Pan Flute, Jazz Flute
2	Clarinet, Organ
3	Violin, Strings
4	Brass, Trumpet
5	Synth Ensemble, Accordion, Brass
6	Pipe Organ, Harpsichord
7	Jazz Organ, Vibraphone, Vibes, Electric Piano, Jazz Guitar
8	Piano, Electric Piano
9	Trumpet, Trombone, Clarinet, Saxophone, Oboe
10	Violin, Cello, Strings